KU-324-592

How societies remember

In treating memory as a cultural rather than an individual faculty, this book provides an account of how practices of a non-inscribed kind are transmitted in, and as, traditions. Most studies of memory as a cultural faculty focus on inscribed transmissions of memories. Connerton, on the other hand, concentrates on incorporated practices, and so questions the currently dominant idea that literary texts may be taken as a metaphor for social practices generally. The author argues that images of the past and recollected knowledge of the past are conveyed and sustained by ritual performances and that performative memory is bodily. Bodily social memory is an essential aspect of social memory, but it is an aspect which has up till now been badly neglected.

An innovative study, this work should be of interest to researchers into social, political and anthropological thought as well as to graduate and undergraduate students.

Themes in the Social Sciences

Editors: John Dunn, Jack Goody, Eugene A. Hammel, Geoffrey Hawthorn

Edmund Leach: *Culture and communication: the logic by which symbols are connected: an introduction to the use of structuralist analysis in social anthropology*

Anthony Heath: *Rational choice and social exchange: a critique of exchange theory*

P. Abrams and A. McCulloch: *Communes, sociology and society*

Jack Goody: *The domestication of the savage mind*

Jean-Louis Flandrin: *Families in former times: kinship, household and sexuality*

John Dunn: *Political theory in the face of the future*

David Thomas: *Naturalism and social science: a post-empiricist philosophy of social science*

Claude Meillassoux: *Maidens, meal and money: capitalism and the domestic community*

David Lane: *Leninism: a sociological interpretation*

Anthony D. Smith: *The ethnic revival*

Jack Goody: *Cooking, cuisine and class: a study in comparative sociology*

Roy Ellen: *Environment, subsistence and system: the ecology of small-scale formations*

S. N. Eisenstadt and L. Roniger: *Patrons, clients and friends: interpersonal relations and the structure of trust in society*

John Dunn: *The politics of socialism: an essay in political theory*

Martine Segalen: *Historical anthropology of the family*

Tim Ingold: *Evolution and social life*

David Levine: *Reproducing families: the political economy of English population history*

Robert Hinde: *Individuals, relationships and culture: links between ethology and the social sciences*

How societies remember

PAUL CONNERTON

CAMBRIDGE
UNIVERSITY PRESS

CAMBRIDGE UNIVERSITY PRESS
Cambridge, New York, Melbourne, Madrid, Cape Town, Singapore, São Paulo, Delhi

Cambridge University Press
The Edinburgh Building, Cambridge CB2 8RU, UK

Published in the United States of America by Cambridge University Press, New York

www.cambridge.org
Information on this title: www.cambridge.org/9780521270939

© Cambridge University Press 1989

This publication is in copyright. Subject to statutory exception
and to the provisions of relevant collective licensing agreements,
no reproduction of any part may take place without
the written permission of Cambridge University Press.

First published 1989
Fifteenth printing 2007

Printed in the United Kingdom at the University Press, Cambridge

A catalogue record for this publication is available from the British Library

Library of Congress Cataloguing in Publication data
Connerton, Paul.
How societies remember.
(Themes in the social sciences)
Bibliography.
Includes index.
1. Memory – Social aspects. 2. Rites and ceremonies –
Psychological aspects. 3. Costume – Psychological aspects.
4. Body, Human – Psychological aspects. 5. Psychohistory.
I. Title. I. Series.
BF378.S65C66 1990 302'.12 89–7070

ISBN 978-0-521-27093-9 paperback

Cambridge University Press has no responsibility for the persistence or accuracy
of URLs for external or third party-internet websites referred to in this publication,
and does not guarantee that any content on such websites is, or will remain,
accurate or appropriate.

Contents

Acknowledgements	*page*	vi
Introduction		1
1 Social memory		6
2 Commemorative ceremonies		41
3 Bodily practices		72
Notes		105
Subject index		116
Name index		119

Acknowledgements

I wish to thank the Director and Deputy Director of the Humanities Research Centre at the Australian National University for the invitation of a Visiting Fellowship and the provision of congenial conditions in which some of the work towards this book was done. I owe a special debt of thanks to Geoffrey Hawthorn, for his steadfast support for this project from its inception as a quite different idea to its eventual appearance as something else, and to Russell Keat, with whom I discussed the details of the work at most stages. The book has benefited from the critical comments on an earlier version of it made by them, and also by Gregory Blue, Nicholas Boyle, Peter Edwards, Ritchie Robertson and Elisabeth Stopp. I am deeply grateful to them all for helping me to say a little more clearly what I wanted to say. Finally, I wish to thank Bobbie Coe and Joyce Leverett who cheerfully and efficiently prepared this manuscript for publication.

Introduction

We generally think of memory as an individual faculty. None the less, there are a number of thinkers who concur in believing that there is some such thing as a collective or social memory.[1] I share that assumption, but tend to diverge over the question as to where this phenomenon, social memory, can be found to be most crucially operative.

Accordingly, the question to which this book is addressed is: how is the memory of groups conveyed and sustained? The term group is here being used in a generously capacious sense and with some flexibility of meaning, to include both small face-to-face societies (such as villages and clubs) and territorially extensive societies most of whose members cannot know each other personally (such as nation-states and world religions).

Readers might reasonably expect that the question thus posed – how is the memory of groups conveyed and sustained? – might lead to a consideration, either of social memory as a dimension of political power, or of the unconscious elements in social memory, or both. In what follows these issues are occasionally touched upon, but they are intentionally not addressed in an explicit and systematic way. The value of addressing such issues, I take it, can hardly be doubted. For it is surely the case that control of a society's memory largely conditions the hierarchy of power; so that, for example, the storage of present-day information technologies, and hence the organisation of collective memory through the use of data-processing machines, is not merely a technical matter but one directly bearing on legitimation, the question of the control and ownership of information being a crucial political issue.[2] Again, the fact that we no longer believe in the great 'subjects' of history – the proletariat, the party, the West – means, not the disappearance of these great master-narratives, but rather their continuing unconscious effectiveness as ways of thinking about and acting in our contemporary situation: their persistence, in other words, as unconscious collective memories.[3]

If neither the politics nor the unconsciousness of memory is explicitly

1

addressed in this book, that is not, therefore, because of any doubts entertained by the author as to their importance, but because what is here being advanced is a different argument: an argument that is not incompatible with holding the positions just indicated, but one which is susceptible of independent investigation. What that investigation intends can perhaps best be indicated by noting at the outset two points that are taken as axiomatic. One concerns memory as such, the other concerns social memory in particular.

Concerning memory as such, we may note that our experience of the present very largely depends upon our knowledge of the past. We experience our present world in a context which is causally connected with past events and objects, and hence with reference to events and objects which we are not experiencing when we are experiencing the present. And we will experience our present differently in accordance with the different pasts to which we are able to connect that present. Hence the difficulty of extracting our past from our present: not simply because present factors tend to influence – some might want to say distort – our recollections of the past, but also because past factors tend to influence, or distort, our experience of the present. This process, it should be stressed, reaches into the most minute and everyday details of our lives. Thus Proust shows us how Marcel's memories of seeing Swann's face were freighted with further memories. For the Swann who in Marcel's youth was a familiar figure in all the fashionable clubs of those days differed largely from the Swann created by Marcel's great-aunt – and hence 'seen' by Marcel – when he appeared in the evenings at Combray; Swann, who was elsewhere in those days so sought after, was treated by Marcel's great-aunt with the rough simplicity of a child who will play with a collector's piece with no more circumspection than if it were some cheap object. From the Swann that Marcel's family had constructed for themselves they had left out, in their ignorance, many details of his life at that time in the fashionable world, details which led other people, when they met him, to see all the graces enshrined in his face. Into this face divested of all glamour Marcel's family implanted a lingering residue made up of their leisurely and companionable hours spent together. Swann's face, his 'corporal envelope', had been so well filled out with this residue of reminiscence that 'their own special Swann' had become to Marcel's family a 'complete and living creature'. Thus even so seemingly simple an act as that which we describe as 'seeing someone we know', Proust reminds us, is to some extent an intellectual process; for we pack the physical outline of the person we see with all the notions we have already formed about them, and in the total picture of them which we compose in our minds those notions have the principal place. In the end 'they come to fill out so completely the curve of his cheeks, to follow so

2

exactly the line of his nose, they blend so harmoniously in the sound of his voice as if it were no more than a transparent envelope, that each time we see the face or hear the voice it is these notions which we recognise and to which we listen'.[4]

Concerning social memory in particular, we may note that images of the past commonly legitimate a present social order. It is an implicit rule that participants in any social order must presuppose a shared memory. To the extent that their memories of a society's past diverge, to that extent its members can share neither experiences nor assumptions. The effect is seen perhaps most obviously when communication across generations is impeded by different sets of memories. Across generations, different sets of memories, frequently in the shape of implicit background narratives, will encounter each other; so that, although physically present to one another in a particular setting, the different generations may remain mentally and emotionally insulated, the memories of one generation locked irretrievably, as it were, in the brains and bodies of that generation. Proust shows us the disconcerting alienation-effect, the sense of a mental jolt, that results from the intersection of incommensurable memories. He shows this in the experience of Marcel, when he returns to fashionable society after a long absence and tries to engage for the first time in conversation with a young American woman who had heard a lot about him from the Duchesse de Guermantes, and who was regarded as one of the most fashionable women of the day but whose name was entirely unknown to Marcel. Conversation with her was agreeable, but for Marcel rendered difficult by the novelty to his ears of the names of most of the people she talked about, although these were the very people who formed the core of polite society at that time. And the converse was also true: at her request Marcel narrated many anecdotes of the past, and many of the names which he pronounced meant nothing to her, she had for the most part never even heard of them. This was not merely because she was young; because she had not lived in France for long and when she first arrived had known nobody, she had only begun to move in fashionable society some years after Marcel had withdrawn from it. Their conversation was unintelligible because the two of them had lived in the same social world but with an interval of twenty-five years. Thus although for ordinary speech she and Marcel used the same language, when it came to names – when it came, we might say, to their seeking to exchange a socially legitimate currency of memories – their vocabularies had nothing in common.[5]

Thus we may say that our experiences of the present largely depend upon our knowledge of the past, and that our images of the past commonly serve to legitimate a present social order. And yet these points, though true, are as they stand insufficient when thus put. For images of the past and recollected knowledge of the past, I want to argue, are conveyed and sustained by (more or less ritual) performances.

In seeking to show how this is the case I shall begin by considering a paradoxical example: that of the French Revolution. It is a paradoxical case because if there is anywhere you would not expect to find social memory at work it must surely be in times of great revolutions. But one thing that tends to get forgotten about the French Revolution is that like all beginnings it involved recollection. Another is that it involved the severing of a head and a change in the clothes people wore. I believe that there is a connection between these two things, and that what we can say about that connection is generalisable beyond the particular instance. I believe, further, that the solution to the question posed above – how is the memory of groups conveyed and sustained? – involves bringing these two things (recollection and bodies) together in a way that we might not have thought of doing.

One might not have thought of doing that because, when recollection has been treated as a cultural rather than as an individual activity, it has tended to be seen as the recollection of a cultural tradition; and such a tradition, in turn, has tended to be thought of as something that is inscribed. More than two millennia – indeed, the whole history of explicit hermeneutic activity – operates in favour of this presupposition. It is true that, for a long time now, the unity of hermeneutics has been seen as residing in the unity of a procedure which is in principle applicable to any object and any practice capable of bearing a meaning. Legal and theological texts, works of art, ritual acts, bodily expressions – all are possible objects of interpretative activity. Yet, although bodily practices are in principle included as possible objects of hermeneutic inquiry, in practice hermeneutics has taken inscription as its privileged object. It arose from and in the course of its history it has constantly returned to the kind of relationship with tradition which focusses on the transmission of what has been inscribed, on texts, or, at the very least, on documentary evidence which is held to have a status comparable to texts, to be constituted, as it were, in the image and likeness of a text.

It is against this antithetical context that I shall seek to give an account of how practices of a non-inscribed kind are transmitted, in and as a tradition. The reader should perhaps be warned as to how this end will be approached. What follows is cast not so much in the form of a treatise as rather in that of an analytical quest; the method is cumulative. Despite the variety of topics that will be discussed, a close logical connection obtains among them. That connection can be expressed by saying that it involved a progressive narrowing of focus. If there is such a thing as social memory, I shall argue, we are likely to find it in commemorative ceremonies; but commemorative ceremonies prove to be commemorative only in so far as they are performative; performativity cannot be thought without a concept of habit; and habit cannot be thought without a notion of bodily automatisms. In this way I shall seek to show that there is an inertia in social structures that is not adequately explained by any of the current orthodoxies of what a social structure is.

1

Social memory

1

All beginnings contain an element of recollection. This is particularly so when a social group makes a concerted effort to begin with a wholly new start. There is a measure of complete arbitrariness in the very nature of any such attempted beginning. The beginning has nothing whatsoever to hold on to; it is as if it came out of nowhere. For a moment, the moment of beginning, it is as if the beginners had abolished the sequence of temporality itself and were thrown out of the continuity of the temporal order. Indeed the actors often register their sense of this fact by inaugurating a new calendar. But the absolutely new is inconceivable. It is not just that it is very difficult to begin with a wholly new start, that too many old loyalties and habits inhibit the substitution of a novel enterprise for an old and established one. More fundamentally, it is that in all modes of experience we always base our particular experiences on a prior context in order to ensure that they are intelligible at all; that prior to any single experience, our mind is already predisposed with a framework of outlines, of typical shapes of experienced objects. To perceive an object or act upon it is to locate it within this system of expectations. The world of the percipient, defined in terms of temporal experience, is an organised body of expectations based on recollection.

In imagining what a historic beginning might be like, the modern imagination has turned back again and again to the events of the French Revolution. This historic rupture, more than any other, has assumed for us the status of a modern myth. It took on that status very quickly. All reflection on history on the continent of Europe throughout the nineteenth century looks behind it to the moment of that revolution in which the meaning of revolution itself was transformed from a circularity of movement to the advent of the new.[1] For those who came after, the present was seen as a time of fall into the ennui of a post-heroic age, or as a permanent

6

state of crisis, the anticipation, whether hoped for or feared, of a recurrent eruption.[2] Revolutionary imagining reached beyond the European heartland; since the late nineteenth century we have lived the myth of the Revolution much as the first Christian generations lived the myth of the End of the World. As early as 1798, Kant remarked that a phenomenon of this kind can never again be forgotten.[3]

Yet this beginning, which provides us with our myth of a historic beginning, serves also, and all the more starkly, to bring into relief the moment of recollection in all apparent beginnings. The work of recollection operated in many ways, explicitly and implicitly, and at many different levels of experience; but I mean to single out here for specific comment the way in which recollection was at work in two distinct areas of social activity: in *commemorative ceremonies* and in *bodily practices*.

2

The beginning which was sought in the trial and execution of Louis XVI of France exhibits this circumstance in a peculiarly dramatic way. The leaders of the Revolution who sat in judgement on Louis faced a problem that was not unique to themselves; it was a problem that confronts any regime, for instance that inaugurated by the Nuremberg Trials, which seeks to establish in a definitive manner the total and complete substitution of a new social order. The regicide of 1793 may be seen as an instance of a more general phenomenon: the trial by fiat of a successor regime. This is unlike any other type of trial. It is different in kind from those that take place under the authority of a long-established regime. It is not like those acts of justice which reinforce a system of retribution by setting its governing principles once more into motion or by modifying the details of their application; it is not a further link in a sequence of settlements through which a regime either achieves greater solidity or moves towards its ultimate disintegration. Those who adhere most resolutely to the principles of the new regime and those who have suffered most severely at the hands of the old regime want not only revenge for particular wrongs and a rectification of particular iniquities. The settlement they seek is one in which the continuing struggle between the new order and the old will be definitively terminated, because the legitimacy of the victors will be validated once and for all. A barrier is to be erected against future transgression. The present is to be separated from what preceded it by an act of unequivocal demarcation. The trial by fiat of a successor regime is like the construction of a wall, unmistakable and permanent, between the new beginnings and the old tyranny. To pass judgement on the practices of the old regime is the constitutive act of the new order.[4]

The trial and execution of Louis XVI was not the murder of a ruler but the revocation of a ruling principle: the principle according to which the dynastic realm was the only imaginable political system. It had indeed been possible to envisage regicide within the terms of that system. For centuries kings had been killed by would-be kings; by private assassins in the pay of would-be kings; or, more rarely, by religious fanatics like the murderers of Henri III and Henri IV of France. But whatever fate might befall individual kings, the principle of dynastic succession remained intact. Whether they died through natural causes or through foul play, the death of kings and the coronation of their successors were comprehensible episodes in the continuum of lineage. Why did the murder of kings leave the institution of kingship untouched? Because, as Camus succinctly put it, none of the murderers ever imagined that the throne might remain empty.[5] No new rulers, that is to say, had ever thought it to be in their interests that the institution of monarchy should be called into question; once crowned, they sought to preserve for themselves the royal authority of the person whose death they had instigated. This form of regicide left the dynastic system unchallenged: the benchmarks of time were still the phases of dynastic rule. The death of a king registered a break in that public time: between one king and another time stood still. There was a gap in it – an interregnum – which people sought to keep as brief as possible. When Louis XVIII of France dated his accession to the throne from the execution of his predecessor, it was to this dynastic principle that he remained true; he was thinking of regicide as it has always been thinkable within the context of the dynastic realm, a context in which assassinations could always be accommodated as episodes within the narrative of dynastic continuity, a context indeed in which assassination was not so much a threat to the power of dynasty as rather an implicit homage to it. Assassination left the principle of the dynastic realm intact because it left unviolated the king as a public person.

The whole point of Louis' trial and execution lay in its ceremonial publicity; it was this that killed him in his public capacity by denying his status as king. The dynastic principle was destroyed not by assassination nor by imprisonment or banishment but by putting Louis, as the embodiment of kingship, to death in such a way that official public abhorrence of the institution of kingship was actually expressed and witnessed.[6] The revolutionaries needed to find some ritual process through which the aura of inviolability surrounding kingship could be explicitly repudiated. What they thus repudiated was not only an institution but the political theology that legitimated that institution.[7] That political theology, the belief that the king united in one person his natural body as an individual and his representative body as the king, was most clearly expressed in the coronation ceremony. It was expressed not in the act of crowning alone but also in the anointing by a bishop of the church, with the all-important phrase announcing that the anointed king rules 'by the grace of God'. It was this double component that gave the coronation rite its quasi-sacramental character. For a thousand years the kings of France had received at their coronation the holy oil as well as the crown upon their heads, after the manner of the apostles' successors. The effect was to transform the enemies of royalty into apparently sacrilegious persons. This was the effect that the public regicide of Louis sought to undo. Here was the oxymoronic element of this regicide: Louis was to be given a royal funeral to end all royal funerals. The ceremony of his trial and execution was intended to exorcise the memory of a prior ceremony. The anointed head was decapitated and the rite of coronation ceremonially revoked. Not simply the natural body of the king but also and above all his political body was killed. In this the actions of the revolutionaries borrowed from the language of the sacred which for so long the dynastic realm had appropriated as its own. Their victim well understood that this was an event in the demise of political theology; Louis XVI, like Charles I of England, explicitly identified himself with the God who died when he spoke of his defeat as a Passion.[5] The proceedings at the trial and execution ceremonially dismantled the sense of sacrilege that had surrounded the murder of kings. One rite revoked another.

A rite revoking an institution only makes sense by invertedly recalling the other rites that hitherto confirmed that institution. The ritual ending of kingship was a settling of accounts with and giving of an account of what it repudiated. The rejection of the principle of the dynastic realm, in this case the ritual enactment of that rejection, was still an account of, and a recalling of, the superseded dynastic realm. The problem here is similar to that which arises over the question of the institution of property. Some people steal from others or defraud them or seize their product. In all these ways they may acquire possessions by means not sanctioned by the prevailing principles of justice in regard to possessions. The existence of past injustice and the continued memory of that injustice raises the question of the rectification of injustices. For if past injustice has shaped the structure of a society's present arrangements for holding property in various ways – or analogously if it is held that past injustice has shaped the structure of a society's arrangements for founding its sovereignty – the question arises as to what now, if anything, ought to be done to rectify these injustices. What kind of criminal blame and what obligations do the performers of past injustice have towards those whose position is worse than it would have been had the injustice not been perpetrated? How far back must you go in taking account of the memory of past injustice, in wiping clean the historical record of illegitimate acts? To construct a barrier between the new beginning and the old tyranny is to recollect the old tyranny.

The styles of clothing characteristic of the revolutionary period celebrated, if not so definitive a beginning, then at least a temporary liberation from the practices of the established order. They mark the attempt to establish a new set of typical *bodily practices*. The participants in the revolution exhibited a form of behaviour that was not unique to themselves: behaviour that is to be found in all carnivals which mark the suspension of hierarchical rank, privileges, norms and prohibitions.[9] Styles of clothing in Paris passed through two phases during the revolutionary period. During the first, which dominated the years 1791–4, clothes became uniforms. The culotte of simple cut and the absence of adornments were emblematic of the desire to eliminate social barriers in the striving for equality: by making the body neutral, citizens were to be free to deal with one another without the intrusion of differences in social status. During the second phase, which dominated the years of Thermidor beginning in 1795, liberty of dress came to mean free bodily movement. People now began to dress in such a way as to expose their bodies to one another on the street and to display the motions of the body. The *merveilleuse*, the woman of fashion, wore light muslin drapery which revealed the shape of the breasts fully and covered neither the arms nor the legs below the knees, while the muslin showed the movement of the limbs when the body changed position. Her male counterpart, the *incroyable*, was a man dressed in the form of a cone with its tip on the ground; very tight trousers led up to short coats and ended in high and exaggerated collars, brightly coloured cravats and hair worn dishevelled or cut close in the style of Roman slaves. While the style of the *merveilleuse* was intended as a liberation in fashion, that of the *incroyable* was meant as sartorial parody; the *incroyable* parodied the Macaronis, stylish dressers of the 1750s, by using lorgnettes and walking with mincing steps. This was a moment in the history of Paris when inhibitory rules were suspended; when, as in all carnival, the people acted out their awareness that established authority was, in reality, a matter of local prescription.[10]

If the revolutionaries rejected the practices of bodily behaviour dominant under the *ancien régime*, that was because they knew that a habit of servitude is incorporated in the behaviour of the servile group by way of their own habits of bodily deportment. This was the point that the deputies of the Third Estate were making when in May 1789 they remonstrated, first at their humiliating official costume, and then, when that had been changed, at the very idea of a costume distinguishing them from the deputies of the nobility. In a pamphlet of 2 May 1789 they attacked the convention requiring the deputies to wear different costumes emblematic of their estate; such a practice, they asserted, perpetuated 'an unacceptable inequality, destructive of the very essence of the Assembly'. What it perpetuated was inequality in an incorporated form: that tradition of bodily practice in accordance with which the upper ranks of society appeared on the street in elaborate costumes which both set them apart from the lower orders and allowed them to dominate the street, a tradition further upheld by sumptuary laws which assigned to each social stratum in the hierarchy a set of appropriate dress and forbade anyone to wear the clothing officially and publicly pronounced suitable for another social rank. The representatives of the Third Estate wanted a licensed transgression, a transgressive act which derived its point not simply from a premeditated beginning for future political activity, but from the exercise of retrospective imagination which recalled a time and a form of social order when appearances on the street were precise indicators of social hierarchy.[11] It has been argued – Burke is the preeminent spokesman of such a view and Oakeshott a recent exemplary exponent – that political ideology must be understood 'not as an independently premeditated beginning for political activity', but as knowledge, in an abstract and generalised form, 'of a concrete manner of attending to the arrangements of society'; that ideologies, as expressed in the form of political programmes or official maxims, can never be more than abbreviations of some manner of concrete behaviour; and that a tradition of behaviour is unavoidably knowledge of detail, since 'what has to be learned is not an abstract idea, or a set of tricks, nor even a ritual, but a concrete, coherent manner of living in all its intricateness'.[12] Such an insight, it is frequently claimed, is exclusive to the true Conservative; but the representatives of the Third Estate, in assigning such importance to the details of everyday dress, showed themselves as aware as their opponents that clothes had the function of saying something about the status of the wearer and, what is equally important, of making that statement a habitual one.

To read or wear clothes is in a significant respect similar to reading or composing a literary text. To read or compose a text as literature, and as belonging to a particular genre of literature, is not to approach it without preconception; one must bring to it an implicit understanding of the operations of literary discourse which tells one what to look for or how to set about composing. Only those who possessed the requisite literary competence would be able to proceed to make sense of a new concatenation of phrases by reading them as literature of a certain type; analogously, only those who possessed the requisite social competence would be able to read the dress of the *incroyable* as a parody of the Macaroni. Just as one group has internalised the grammar of literature which enables

11

them to convert linguistic sentences into literary structures and meanings, so likewise has the other internalised the grammar of dress which enables them to convert clothing items into clothing structures and meanings. Anyone who does not possess such competences, anyone unfamiliar with the conventions by which fictions are read or people clothed, would, for example, be quite puzzled if confronted with a lyric poem or a person dressed in the style of an *incroyable*. In reading literature one assigns the object in question to a genre; in interpreting clothes one proceeds likewise. An individual literary feature, or an individual clothing feature, possesses meaning because it is perceived as part of a whole cluster of meanings; and, in each case, this type of whole must be a more or less explicit guess about the kind of utterance or the kind of dress that is being interpreted. Unless interpreters make a guess about the kind of meaning they confront they have no way of unifying their transient encounters with the details. And this subsumption of the particular experience under a type or genre is not simply a process of identifying certain explicit features. It also entails a set of expectations by virtue of which one believes that many of the unexamined features in the new experience will be the same as features characteristic of previous experience; or, if they are not the same, that they are describable in terms of their degree of divergence from that set of expectations. This structure of implicit expectations is always a component of a type – a type of literature or a type of clothing – because it is by virtue of them that a new instance can be subsumed before it is completely known.[13]

In the two cases just looked at – that of ceremonial trial and execution, and that of newly developed practices of clothing – we find a common feature. The attempt to break definitively with an older social order encounters a kind of historical deposit and threatens to founder upon it. The more total the aspirations of the new regime, the more imperiously will it seek to introduce an era of forced forgetting. To say that societies are self-interpreting communities is to indicate the nature of that deposit; but it is important to add that among the most powerful of these self-interpretations are the images of themselves as continuously existing that societies create and preserve. For an individual's consciousness of time is to a large degree an awareness of society's continuity, or more exactly of the image of that continuity which the society creates. I have suggested, with respect to the French Revolution, that at least part of this deposit is to be found in repeated commemorative acts and at least part in culturally specific bodily practices. That deposit was composed, in regard to the ceremony of regicide, of feelings with respect to the king, or rather towards his kingship, that bore the mark of ancient beliefs with roots in old religions and ways of thought that left behind a sense of the inviolate and inviolable; that is why the public execution of Louis was felt by all his contemporaries to be so awesome an event. And it was composed, in regard to the clothing practices of the early revolutionary period and Thermidor, of hierarchic prescriptions that were incorporated in habitual bodily practices; that is why the new fashions of the 1790s were experienced by the participants as such a heady release. Regicide was a ritual revocation, sartorial licence was a carnival liberation. In both types of action we see people trying to mark out the boundaries of a radical beginning; and in neither case is that beginning, that new image of society's continuity, even thinkable without its element of recollection – of recollection both explicit and implicit. The attempt to establish a beginning refers back inexorably to a pattern of social memories.

3

We need to distinguish *social memory* from a more specific practice that is best termed the activity of *historical reconstruction*. Knowledge of all human activities in the past is possible only through a knowledge of their traces. Whether it is the bones buried in Roman fortifications, or a pile of stones that is all that remains of a Norman tower, or a word in a Greek inscription whose use or form reveals a custom, or a narrative written by the witness of some scene, what the historian deals with are traces: that is to say the marks, perceptible to the senses, which some phenomenon, in itself inaccessible, has left behind. Just to apprehend such marks as traces of something, as evidence, is already to have gone beyond the stage of merely making statements about the marks themselves; to count something as evidence is to make a statement about something else, namely, about that for which it is taken as evidence.

Historians, that is to say, proceed inferentially. They investigate evidence much as lawyers cross-question witnesses in a court of law, extracting from that evidence information which it does not explicitly contain or even which was contrary to the overt assertions contained in it. Those parts of the evidence which are made up of previous statements are in no sense privileged; a previous statement claiming to be true has for the historian the same status as any other type of evidence. Historians are able to reject something explicitly told them in their evidence and to substitute their own interpretation of events in its place. And even if they do accept what a previous statement tells them, they do this not because that statement exists and is taken as authoritative but because it is judged to satisfy the historian's criteria of historical truth. Far from relying on authorities other than themselves, to whose statements their thought must conform, historians are their own authority; their thought is autonomous vis-à-vis their evidence, in the sense that they possess criteria by reference to which that evidence is criticised.[14]

Historical reconstruction is thus not dependent on social memory. Even when no statement about an event or custom has reached the historian by an unbroken tradition from eyewitnesses, it is still possible for the historian to rediscover what has been completely forgotten. Historians can do this partly by the critical examination of statements contained in their written sources, where written sources mean sources containing statements asserting or implying alleged facts regarding the subject in which the historian is interested, and partly by the use of what are called unwritten sources, for example archaeological material connected with the same subject, the point of describing these as unwritten sources being to indicate that, since they are not texts, they contain no ready-made statements.

But historical reconstruction is still necessary even when social memory preserves direct testimony of an event. For if a historian is working on a problem in recent history and receives at first hand a ready-made answer to the very question being put to the evidence, then the historian will need to question that statement if it is to be considered as evidence; and this is the case even if the answer which the historian receives is given by an eye-witness or by the person who did what the historian is inquiring into. Historians do not continue to question the statements of their informants because they think that the informants want to deceive them or have themselves been deceived. Historians continue to question the statements of their informants because if they were to accept them at face value that would amount to abandoning their autonomy as practising historians. They would then have relinquished their independence of social memory: an independence based on their claim to have the right to make up their own mind, by methods proper to their own science, as to the correct solution of the problems that arise in the course of that scientific practice.

Despite this independence from social memory, the practice of historical reconstruction can in important ways receive a guiding impetus from, and can in turn give significant shape to, the memory of social groups. A particularly extreme case of such interaction occurs when a state apparatus is used in a systematic way to deprive its citizens of their memory. All totalitarianisms behave in this way; the mental enslavement of the subjects of a totalitarian regime begins when their memories are taken away. When a large power wants to deprive a small country of its national consciousness it uses the method of organised forgetting. In Czech history alone this organised oblivion has been instituted twice, after 1618 and after 1948. Contemporary writers are proscribed, historians are dismissed from their posts, and the people who have been silenced and removed from their jobs become invisible and forgotten. What is horrifying in totalitarian regimes is not only the violation of human dignity but the fear that there might remain nobody who could ever again properly bear witness to the past. Orwell's evocation of a form of government is acute not least in its apprehension of this state of collective amnesia. Yet it later turns out – in reality, if not in *Nineteen Eighty-Four* – that there were people who realised that the struggle of citizens against state power is the struggle of their memory against forced forgetting, and who made it their aim from the beginning not only to save themselves but to survive as witnesses to later generations, to become relentless recorders: the names of Solzhenitsyn and Wiesel must stand for many. In such circumstances their writing of oppositional histories is not the only practice of documented historical reconstruction; but precisely because it is that it preserves the memory of social groups whose voice would otherwise have been silenced.

Again, the historiography of the Crusades is eloquent testimony to the role of historical writing in the formation of political identity. Medieval Muslim historians did not share with medieval European Christians the sense of witnessing a great struggle between Islam and Christendom for the control of the Holy Land. In the extensive Muslim historiography of that time the words 'Crusade' and 'Crusader' never occur. The contemporary Muslim historians spoke of the Crusaders either as the Infidels or as the Franks, and they viewed the attacks launched by them in Syria, Egypt and Mesopotamia, between the end of the eleventh and the end of the thirteenth centuries, as being in no way fundamentally different from the former wars waged between Islam and the Infidels: in Syria itself in the course of the tenth century and before, in Andalus throughout the Spanish Reconquista, and in Sicily against the Normans. A history of the Crusades cannot be found in the Muslim historical writing of that time; it contains at most only fragments of what such a history might be, embedded in treatises on other subjects. Medieval Muslim historiography is only incidentally a history of the Crusades. But in the period since 1945 an expanding body of Arabic historical writing has taken the Crusades as its theme. The Crusades have now become a code word for the malign intentions of the Western powers. Muslim historians have come to see a certain parallelism between the period of the twelfth and thirteenth centuries and the last hundred years. In both cases the Islamic Middle East was assailed by European forces which succeeded in imposing their control upon a large part of the region. From a Muslim viewpoint, the Crusades have come to be seen as the primary phase of European colonisation, the prefiguration of a long-term movement which includes the Buonaparte expedition, the British conquest of Egypt, and the Mandate system in the Levant. That movement is seen as culminating in the foundation of the

15

state of Israel: and with each ensuing struggle – the Arab–Israel War of 1948, the Suez War, the Six Day War – the Muslim study of the Crusades gained momentum. Muslim historians now see in the rise and fall of the Crusader principalities parallels to contemporary events. The Crusaders, who crossed the sea and established an independent state in Palestine, have become proto-Zionists.[15]

A more paradoxical case still is that presented by the transformation of historical writing in the nineteenth century. The paradox lies in two antithetical yet equally essential aspects of this process as it was interpreted by those who were caught up in it. One view of this intellectual enterprise fastens attention upon the privileged status of the historical sciences. This way of seeing things depends upon isolating the practice of methodical understanding that takes place in the historical sciences from a more all-embracing phenomenon, the processes of interpretation that occur implicitly and everywhere in the course of everyday life. And this leads on to a sense that the practice of historical research is creating a new distance from the past by setting people free from the tradition that might otherwise have guided their assumptions and behaviour. A historically tutored memory is opposed to an unreflective traditional memory.[16] And yet another sense of this same enterprise acknowledges that it is unthinkable outside its setting within the broader context of a struggle for political identity. It is part of the history of nationalism. For the transformation of the writing of history is in large part the work of the great German scholars, Niebuhr and Savigny, Ranke and Mommsen, Troeltsch and Meinecke, all of whom were intimately involved with the life of the political society to which they belonged. They rejected any form of political universalism and in particular the principles of 1789 which claimed to establish rules of common life and of participation in the activities of the state which were valid, in principle, for all peoples; and they affirmed, in opposition to this, the value of treating law, not as socially constructed machinery, but as the embodiment and expression of a nation's continuity. Whether they were writing about their own times or about distant cultures, it is this political commitment of these major figures of the historical school which imparts to their work the sense that, in constructing a canon of historical research, they are at the same time participating in the formation of a political identity and giving shape to the memory of a particular culture.[17]

In these cases, whether the activity of historical reconstruction is systematically repressed or whether it flourishes expansively, it leads to the production of formal, written histories. There is, however, a phenomenon more procedurally informal and more culturally diffused than the activity of producing histories understood in this sense. The production of more or less *informally* told narrative histories turns out to be a basic activity for characterisation of human actions. It is a feature of all communal memory.

Consider the case of village life. What is lacking in a village setting is not simply the physical space but the performative space which we habitually negotiate in an urban context. We are accustomed to moving in a milieu of strangers where many of the people who witness the actions and declarations of others usually have little or no knowledge of their history and little or no experience of similar actions and declarations in their past. This is what makes it difficult to judge whether, or how far, a particular person is to be believed in a given situation. If we are to play a believable role before an audience of relative strangers we must produce or at least imply a history of ourselves: an informal account which indicates something of our origins and which justifies or perhaps excuses our present status and actions in relation to that audience.[18] But this presentation of the self in everyday life is unnecessary when, as is the case in the life of a village, the gaps in shared memory are much fewer and slighter. In Proust's village of Combray a person whom one 'didn't know from Adam' was as incredible a being as a mythological deity, and on the various occasions when one of these startling apparitions had occurred in the Rue du Saint-Esprit or in the Square, no one could remember exhaustive inquiries ever having failed to reduce the fabulous creature to the proportions of a person whom one 'did know', if not personally then at least in the abstract, as being more or less closely related to some family in Combray.[19] *The Return of Martin Guerre* highlights the same feature from a reverse angle. The startling apparition of the chief protagonist, who can do no more than pretend to belong, is the ultimate anomaly in a setting where deceit is rare and never on a large scale because the space between what is generally known about a person and what is unknown about them is too slight for self-interest and guile to lead to the performance of a role. What holds this space together is gossip. Most of what happens in a village during the course of a day will be recounted by somebody before the day ends and these reports will be based on observation or on first-hand accounts. Village gossip is composed of this daily recounting combined with lifelong mutual familiarities. By this means a village informally constructs a continuous communal history of itself: a history in which everybody portrays, in which everybody is portrayed, and in which the act of portrayal never stops. This leaves little if any space for the presentation of the self in everyday life because, to such a large degree, individuals remember in common.[20]

Or again, if we consider the political education of ruling groups, we cannot fail to be struck by the distinction between their political records and their political memories. The ruling group will use its knowledge of the past in a direct and active way.[21] Its political behaviour and decisions will be based on an investigation of the past, especially the recent past, conducted by its police, its research bureaux and its administrative services, and these investigations will be carried out with an efficiency which is later occasionally revealed to those concerned when documents come to light following a war, a revolution, or a public scandal. But one of the limitations of documentary evidence is that few people bother to write down what they take for granted. And yet much political experience will have been built up about 'what goes without saying', and this may be particularly easy to observe in a fairly technical sphere like that of diplomacy or in the dealings of a close-knit governing class. In this sense, and it is an important one, the political records of the ruling group are far from exhausting its political memory. The distinction becomes particularly evident when its leaders have to take decisions in crises which they cannot wholly understand and where the outcome of their actions is impossible to foresee; for it is then that they will have recourse to certain rules and beliefs which 'go without saying', when their actions are directed by an implicit background narrative which they take for granted. Thus throughout the eighteenth century statesmen went on believing that, above all things, they must prevent any further power from ever achieving an ascendancy like that of Louis XIV; and they would remind themselves that nothing like the old wars of religion must be allowed to recur.[22] Throughout the nineteenth century it was common to interpret every violent upheaval in terms of the continuation of the movement begun in 1789, so that the times of restoration appeared as pauses during which the revolutionary current had gone underground only to break through to the surface once more, and on the occasion of each upheaval, in 1830 and 1832, in 1848 and 1851, in 1871, adherents and opponents of the revolution alike understood the events as immediate consequences of 1789.[23] Again, if we are to understand the assumptions of 1914, we need to appreciate the links between the values and beliefs inculcated at school and the presuppositions on which politicians acted in later life; it is to the ideas of a generation earlier that we must attend if we are to appreciate how literally the doctrine of the struggle for existence and the survival of the fittest was taken by many European leaders just before the First World War.[24]

Or consider the case of life histories. After all, most people do not belong to ruling élites or experience the history of their own lives primarily in the context of the life of such élites. For some time now a generation of mainly socialist historians have seen in the practice of oral history the possibility of rescuing from silence the history and culture of subordinate groups. Oral histories seek to give voice to what would otherwise remain voiceless even if not traceless, by reconstituting the life histories of individuals. But to think the concept of a life history is already to come to the matter with a mental set, and so it sometimes happens that the line of questioning adopted by oral historians impedes the realisation of their intentions. Oral historians frequently report the occurrence of a characteristic type of difficulty at the beginning of their conversations. The interviewee hesitates and is silent, protests that there is nothing to relate which the interviewer does not already know. The historian will only exacerbate the difficulty if the interviewee is encouraged to embark on a form of chronological narrative. For this imports into the material a type of narrative shape, and with that a pattern of remembering, that is alien to that material. In suggesting this the interviewer is unconsciously adjusting the life history of the interviewee to a preconceived and alien model. That model has its origin in the culture of the ruling group; it derives from the practice of more or less famous citizens who write memoirs towards the end of their lives. These writers of memoirs see their life as worth remembering because they are, in their own eyes, someone who has taken decisions which exerted, or can be represented as having exerted, a more or less wide influence and which have visibly changed part of their social world. The 'personal' history of the memoir writer has confronted an 'objective' history embodied in institutions, or in the modification or transformation or even overthrow of institutions: a programme of educational training, a pattern of civil administration, a legal system, a particular organisation of the division of labour. They have been inserted into the structure of dominant institutions and have been able to turn that structure to their own ends. It is this perceived capacity of making a personal intervention that makes it possible for the writers of memoirs to conceive their life retrospectively, and frequently to envisage it prospectively, as a narrative sequence in which they are able to integrate their individual life history with their sense of the course of an objective history. But what is lacking in the life histories of those who belong to subordinate groups is precisely those terms of reference that conduce to and reinforce this sense of a linear trajectory, a sequential narrative shape: above all, in relation to the past, the notion of legitimating origins, and in relation to the future, the sense of an accumulation in power or money or influence. The oral history of subordinate groups will produce another type of history: one in which not only will most of the details be different, but in which the very construction of meaningful shapes will obey a different principle. Different details will emerge because they are inserted, as it were, into a different kind of narrative home. For it is essential in perceiving the existence of a culture of subordinate groups to see that this is a culture in which the life histories of its members have a different rhythm and that this rhythm is not patterned by the individual's intervention in the working of the dominant institutions.

When oral historians listen carefully to what their informants have to say they discover a perception of time that is not linear but cyclical. The life of the interviewee is not a curriculum vitae but a series of cycles. The basic cycle is the day, then the week, the month, the season, the year, the generation. The remarkable success in the United States of Studs Terkel's *Working* no doubt stems from the fact that it does justice to this alternative cyclical form and can be read as popular epic as well as social research. Here is a different narrative shape, a different socially determined structuring of memories.[25]

Even so fundamental a question as what the shape of the twentieth century looks like will depend crucially upon what social group we happen to belong to. For many people, but especially for Europeans, the narrative of this century is unthinkable without the memory of the Great War. The image of the trenches from the Channel to the Swiss border is engraved in modern memory. Whereas in the Second World War the common experiences of soldiers was dire long-term exile at an unbridgeable distance from home, what makes the experience of the Great War unique, and what gives it a special burden of irony, is the absurd proximity of the trenches to home. This entrenched experience, of which the first day on the Somme is emblematic, stands like a narrative archetype. Paul Fussell has vividly evoked this primal scene and suggested that it is its particular ironic structure, its dynamic of hope abridged, that makes it haunt the memory.[26] And yet – this is the remarkable thing – it is possible to imagine that the members of two quite different groups may participate in the same event, even so catastrophic and all-engulfing an event as a great war, but still these two groups may be to such a degree incommensurable that their subsequent memories of that event, the memories they pass on to their children, can scarcely be said to refer to the 'same' event. Carlo Levi has given a remarkable insight into this phenomenon.[27] In 1935 he was exiled as a political prisoner to the remote village of Gagliano in Southern Italy. On the wall of the town hall there was a marble stone inscribed with the names of all the villagers of Gagliano who had died in the Great War. There were almost fifty names; directly or through ties to cousinship or *comparaggio* not a single household had been spared; and besides, there were those who had returned from the war wounded and those who had returned safe and sound. As a doctor, Levi soon had occasion to talk to all the villagers, and he was curious to learn how they viewed the cataclysm of 1914–18. And yet, in all his talks with the peasants of Gagliano, nobody ever mentioned the war, to speak of deeds accomplished or places seen or sufferings endured. Not that the subject was taboo; when questioned on the matter they answered not only briefly but with indifference. They neither remembered the war as a remarkable event nor spoke of its dead.

But of one war they spoke constantly. This was the war of the brigands. Brigandage had come to an end in 1865, seventy years before; very few of the peasants were old enough to remember it, as participants or eye-witnesses. Yet everyone, young as well as old, women as well as men, spoke of it as if it were yesterday. The adventures of the brigands entered easily into their everyday speech and were commemorated in the names of many sites in and around the village. The only wars the peasants of Gagliano spoke of with animation and mythic coherence were the sporadic outbursts of revolt in which the brigands had fought against the army and the government of the north. But of the motives and interests at play in the World War they were barely conscious. The Great War was not part of their memory.

Thus we may say, more generally, that we all come to know each other by asking for accounts, by giving accounts, by believing or disbelieving stories about each other's pasts and identities.[28] In successfully identifying and understanding what someone else is doing we set a particular event or episode or way of behaving in the context of a number of narrative histories. Thus we identify a particular action by recalling at least two types of context for that action. We situate the agents' behaviour with reference to its place in their life history; and we situate that behaviour also with reference to its place in the history of the social settings to which they belong. The narrative of one life is part of an interconnecting set of narratives; it is embedded in the story of those groups from which individuals derive their identity.

4

There is a striking disparity between the pervasiveness of social memory in the conduct of everyday life and the relatively scant attention, at least as regards explicit and systematic as distinct from implicit and scattered treatment, that has been paid to specifically *social* memory in modern social and cultural theory.[29] Why is this so?

The answer is a rather complicated one, and we must begin by noting that one of the chief difficulties in developing a theory of memory as a form of cognition has to do with the variety of kinds of memory claims that we make and acknowledge. The verb 'remember' enters into a variety of grammatical constructions and the things that are remembered are of many different kinds; and if memory as a specifically social phenomenon has suffered relative neglect, that is at least in part because certain types of memory claims have been privileged as the focus of certain types of extended attention. It will be helpful, then, to distinguish in particular between three distinct classes of memory claim.

There is, first, a class of *personal* memory claims. These refer to those acts of remembering that take as their object one's life history. We speak of them as personal memories because they are located in and refer to a personal past. My personal memory claims may be expressed in the form: I did such and such, at such and such a time, in such and such a place. Thus in remembering an event I am also concerned with my own self. When I say 'I arrived in Rome three years ago', I am in a certain sense reflecting upon myself. In making that statement I am aware of my actual present, and I reflect on myself as the one who did this and that in the past. In remembering that I did this and that I see myself, as it were, from a distance. There is a kind of doubling: I, who speak now, and I, who arrived in Rome three years ago, are in some ways identical but in some ways different. These memory claims figure significantly in our self-descriptions because our past history is an important source of our conception of ourselves; our self-knowledge, our conception of our own character and potentialities, is to a large extent determined by the way in which we view our own past actions. There is, then, an important connection between the concept of personal identity and various backward-looking mental states; thus, the appropriate objects of remorse or guilt are past actions or omissions done by the person who feels remorseful or guilty. Through memories of this kind, persons have a special access to facts about their own past histories and their own identities, a kind of access that in principle they cannot have to the histories and identities of other persons and things.[30]

A second group of memory claims – *cognitive* memory claims – covers uses of 'remember' where we may be said to remember the meaning of words, or lines of verse, or jokes, or stories, or the lay-out of a city, or mathematical equations, or truths of logic, or facts about the future. To have memory knowledge of this kind one's knowledge must in some way be due to, must exist because of, a past cognitive or sensory state of oneself;[31] but – unlike the first class of memory claims – we need not possess any information about the context or episode of learning in order to be able to retain and use memories of this class. What this type of remembering requires is, not that the object of memory be something that is past, but that the person who remembers that thing must have met, experienced or learned of it in the past.

A third class of memories consists simply in our having the capacity to reproduce a certain performance. Thus remembering how to read or how to write or how to ride a bicycle is in each case a matter of our being able to do these things, more or less effectively, when the need to do so arises. As with experiential and cognitive memory claims, it is part of the meaning of 'remembers' that what is remembered is past; 'remembers', we might say, is a past-referring term. But as regards this third class of memories, we frequently do not recall how or when or where we have acquired the knowledge in question; often it is only by the fact of the performance that we are able to recognise and demonstrate to others that we do in fact remember. The memory of how to read or write or ride a bicycle is like the meaning of a lesson thoroughly learned; it has all the marks of a habit, and the better we remember this class of memories, the less likely it is that we will recall some previous occasion on which we did the thing in question; it is only when we find ourselves in difficulties that we may turn to our recollections as a guide.

Philosophers have acknowledged the existence of this class of memory claims and have grouped them under the heading of '*habit-memory*', in contrast to personal and cognitive memory. But they have normally paid little attention to memory claims of this type. They have often argued or assumed that in 'true' memory the remembering itself, as well as what is remembered, is always a certain kind of event; remembering is frequently said to be a 'mental act' or 'mental occurrence'. Thus Bergson distinguishes two sorts of memory, the kind that consists of habit and the kind that consists of recollection. He gives the example of learning a lesson by heart. When I know the lesson by heart I am said to 'remember' it; but this only means that I have acquired certain habits. On the other hand, my recollection of the first time I read the lesson while I was learning it is the recollection of a unique event which occurred only once, and the recollection of a unique event cannot wholly be constituted by habit and is radically different from the memory that is habit. This leads Bergson to conclude that the memory of how to do something is simply the retention of a 'motor mechanism' and that this 'habit-memory' is radically different from the recollection of unique events that is 'memory *par excellence*'; this type of recollection alone is said to be memory proper.[32] Russell follows Bergson in distinguishing between 'habit-memory' and 'true memory', the latter being cognitive while the former is not. He does indeed acknowledge that it is more difficult to apply this distinction in practice than it is to draw it in theory. The reason for this is that habit is an intrusive feature of our mental life and is often present where at first sight it appears not to be. Thus there can be a habit of remembering a unique event; when we have once described the event, the words we have used to do so can easily become habitual. Nevertheless, Russell wants to insist that the distinctive characteristic of memory is that it is a certain special kind of belief. What constitutes 'knowledge-memory', he argues, is 'our belief' that 'images of past occurrences refer to past occurrences'. He speaks of this as 'true' memory in order to distinguish it from mere habit acquired through past experience.[33] Here again, it is the sense of 'remember' in which remembering is a cognitive act that is taken to be of philosophical importance.

23

It is perhaps easier to appreciate the significance of the range of behaviour commonly assigned to the class of habit-memories by examining cases of amnesia in which such memory capacities no longer operate effectively, rather than by noting the more or less smooth operation of such capacities in the course of everyday life. And we are fortunate in having a study, by the distinguished neurophysiologist Luria, which reports one remarkable case of such amnesia and which, in documenting this, demonstrates just how extensive and vital habit memory is.[34] It concerns the history of a brain wound suffered by a Russian soldier, Zazetsky, of the state of psychological disorder in which he was forced to live after irreparable damage had been done by a bullet that penetrated his brain and of his struggle to piece together an account of his state of psychological disarray and to combat it.

He suffered a devastating loss of personal memory. During the weeks immediately after his injury he was unable to remember his first name, his patronymic, the names of his close relatives or the name of his home town, and he had a great deal of trouble remembering anything about his recent past – even what life had been like at the front.

Equally devastating was his loss of cognitive memory. He had difficulty in identifying things in his environment. When he saw or imagined things – physical objects, plants, animals, birds, people – he could not immediately recall the words for them. And vice versa: when he heard a word he could not remember right away what it meant. This cognitive loss was syntactic as well as semantic. We express relationships through certain parts of speech – prepositions, conjunctions, adverbs, and so on – so that simple phrases like 'the basket under the table' and 'the cross above the circle' are perfectly obvious to us because we assume the faculty necessary to master such forms: the ability to remember grammatical elements and to perceive, quickly and simultaneously, the relationships of individual words and images which they evoke. But Zazetsky no longer had the capacity for such instantaneous grasp of patterns; and there were some grammatical patterns – for instance, inversions like that in the distinction between 'mother's brother' and 'brother's mother', or referred genitives as in 'father's brother' – that he could no longer grasp at all.

A third area of loss had to do with habitual patterns of behaviour. While he was in hospital he discovered that he had to relearn what had once been commonplace: to beckon to someone or to wave goodbye. He was lying in bed and needed the nurse. How was he to get her to come over? Suddenly he remembered that you can beckon to someone and he tried to beckon to the nurse: that is, to move his left hand lightly back and forth. But she walked past and paid no attention to his gesturing. He realised then that he had completely forgotten how to beckon to someone. It appeared that he had even forgotten how to gesture with his hands so that someone

24

could understand what he meant. When a doctor wanted to shake hands with him, he did not know which hand to extend. When an instructor gave him a needle, a spool of thread, and some material with a pattern on it, and asked him to try to stitch the pattern, he simply sat with the needle, thread and material considering why he had been given these; when the instructor later returned and told him to thread the needle, he took the needle in one hand and the thread in the other, but could not understand what to do with them. When he went to a workshop to learn shoemaking, the instructor explained everything to him in great detail; but all he learnt to do was to drive wooden nails into a board and pull them out again. If later he wanted to do some simple everyday task around the house, and he was asked to chop wood, or mend the fence, or fetch some milk from the storeroom, he found he did not know how to proceed. If we are to give a name to this drastic area of loss, what can we call it but habit-memory?

5

Of the three types of memory that I have distinguished, the first two, personal and cognitive memory, have been studied in detail but by quite different methods, while the third, habit-memory, has for important reasons been largely ignored.

Central to the study of memory as understood in psychoanalysis is the distinction between two contrasting ways of bringing the past into the present: acting out and remembering.[35] Acting out consists in a type of action in which the subject, in the grip of unconscious wishes and fantasies, relives these in the present with an impression of immediacy which is heightened by the analysand's refusal or inability to acknowledge their origin and, therefore, their repetitive character. The behaviour of acting out generally displays a compulsive aspect which is at odds with the rest of the analysand's behaviour patterns. Often it takes the form of aggressive behaviour which may be directed against others or against the self. From the explanatory point of view, the crucial point is that acting out, whether violent or subdued, whether directed against others or against the self, and whether it occurs outside or within the relationship between analyst and analysand, is evidence of the compulsion to repeat. It is as a result of this compulsion to repeat that analysands deliberately place themselves in distressing situations: in this way repeating an old experience. But in compulsive repetition the agents fail to remember the prototype of their present actions. On the contrary, they have the strong impression that the situations in which they are 'caught up' are fully determined by the circumstances of the moment. The compulsion to repeat has replaced the capacity to remember. 'The patient repeats instead of remembering and repeats under the condition of resistance': the formula occurs in a text crucial for analytic technique, Freud's 1914 essay on 'Remembering, repeating, and working through'.[36]

It is at this point, in his essay of 1914, that Freud introduces the topic of transference: a phenomenon which he discusses mainly in terms of the relation between analyst and analysand because, although certainly not confined to this relation, the behaviour of acting out is observable directly and in great detail within the analytical space. He describes transference as the main instrument 'for curbing the patient's compulsion to repeat and for turning it into a motive for remembering'. Why should transference have this effect? If remembering is to be made free to occur, this, says Freud, is because the transference constitutes something like a 'playground' in which the patient's compulsion to repeat 'is allowed to expand in almost complete freedom'. Extending this analogy of the playground, he says that the transference sets up 'an intermediate realm between illness and real life through which the transition from the one to the other is made'. This intermediate realm consists to a very large extent of narrative activity: the analysands tell of their past, of their present life outside the analysis, of their life within the analysis. Freud never explicitly discussed this narrative character of the analytic experience; but later writers, for instance Sherwood and Spence, have pointed to its central importance and have shown the ways in which the psychoanalytic dialogue seeks to uncover the analysand's efforts to maintain in existence a particular kind of narrative discontinuity.[37] The point of this narrative discontinuity is to block out parts of a personal past and, thereby, not only of a personal past, but also of significant features of present actions. In order to discard this radical discontinuity, psychoanalysis works in a temporal circle: analyst and analysand work backwards from what is told about the autobiographical present in order to reconstruct a coherent account of the past; while, at the same time, they work forwards from various tellings about the autobiographical past in order to reconstitute that account of the present which it is sought to understand and explain. Accordingly, there is a rule of thumb in Freud's technical writings which advises the analyst to direct attention to the past when the analysand insists upon the present, and to look for present material when the analysand dwells on the past. One set of narratives is deployed to generate questions about another set of narratives. To remember, then, is precisely not to recall events as isolated; it is to become capable of forming meaningful narrative sequences. In the name of a particular narrative commitment, an attempt is being made to integrate isolated or alien phenomena into a single unified process. This is the sense in which psychoanalysis sets itself the task of reconstituting individual life histories.

Central to the study of cognitive memory, that is to say memory as understood by experimental psychologists, is the notion of encoding.[38] They have shown that literal recall is very rare and unimportant, remembering being not a matter of reproduction but of construction; it is the construction of a 'schema', a coding, which enables us to distinguish and, therefore, to recall. Three major dimensions of mnemonic coding are known to experimental psychologists today. The semantic code is the dominant dimension; like a library code, it is organised hierarchically by topic and integrated into a single system according to an overall view of the world and the logical relationships perceived in it. The verbal code is the second dimension; it contains all the information and programmes that allow the preparation of a verbal expression. The visual code is the third dimension; concrete items easily translated into images are much better retained than abstract items because such concrete items undergo a double encoding in terms of visual coding as well as verbal expression. Experimental psychologists explain failures of memory in terms of the operation of such coding processes; and this explanation holds for pathological as well as for normal cases. As an example of normal forgetting we might consider those cases where events and situations of a repetitive nature are not easily recalled. Any time I go to buy bread is like the last time, except for the day; in such situations only the first and the last experiences will be remembered, so that the ability to recall any given instance typically assumes the shape of a U-curve; all intermediate instances will be forgotten because their labels are practically identical. As an example of pathological forgetting we might consider the case of patients who suffer amnesia concerning the names of colours.[39] The fact that patients who suffer from colour amnesia are unable to 'see at a glance' which colour samples presented to them 'go together' is a specific manifestation of a more general disorder; it is a sign of the fact that they have lost the general ability to subsume a sense datum under a category. For to name a thing is to see it as representative of a category. Hence it would be wrong to say that people manifesting colour amnesia move from one principle of classification to another because they are unable to adhere to a given principle of classification; in reality, they never adopt any principle of classification.

Experimental psychologists have been concerned to understand the phenomena of remembering and forgetting as part of a deliberately scientific enterprise: the quest for a fundamental understanding of the brain and sensory apparatus viewed as a system capable of selecting, organising, storing and retrieving information. They take the view that the foundations of such understanding are to be laid through rigorously designed experiments carried out under highly controlled and thus, on the whole, highly artificial conditions. Thus in the course of experiments on memory the experimental subject is generally presented with material belonging to two main groups: verbal and non-verbal material. Verbal material will commonly include series of names, adjectives, verbs, prose passages, poems and stories. Non-verbal material will commonly include geometrical shapes such as circles, squares and rectangles, as well as drawings, paintings and photographs of people, objects and scenes. In order to be able to describe and classify the performances of their experimental subjects, cognitive psychologists will place those subjects in experimental situations which have been as far as possible emptied of specific cultural content. Cognitive psychologists can indeed acknowledge, without prejudice to their premises, that the memories of people in different cultures will vary because their mental maps are different. The semantic code, which is the key to the whole operation of memory, is a mental map acquired in childhood, and, as such, it is a code that is shared collectively. Thus it can be readily admitted that in most cultures the memories of men and women will vary because their education and occupations are different; and it can be as easily conceded that witnesses from sharply differing cultures will inevitably differ in their recollections of the same event, particularly if that is a complex event like most of those to which oral traditions allude. In making such acknowledgements experimental psychologists are admitting the possible application of their findings to socially variable object-domains. But what their research has basically been concerned to explore is the existence and universality of basic cognitive structures; what they seek to identify are 'fundamental structures', 'primary processes', 'universals', mental faculties that are essential to human nature.

Here, then, we have two heavily colonised territories. Psychoanalysts have studied personal memory in the course of investigating the *life histories of individuals*, whereas psychologists have studied cognitive memory in the course of investigating the workings of *universal mental faculties*. Habit-memory, by contrast, appears to be an unoccupied or even non-existent space. Or perhaps it would be better to say that the intellectual space that might be occupied by a theory of habit is already occupied. The ground which it might cover appears to be already occupied by contemporary *conventionalism*. For if they now agree on little else, everyone agrees that social worlds are defined by their ruling conventions. With the idea of convention we explain to ourselves the notion of an order of objective rules at whose base lies a tacit social dimension, a world taken to be the world that it is because the rules that make it what it is are intersubjectively agreed. And language has become for us the archetypal model for all other forms of intersubjectivity, because language has its roots on the one hand in the nature of formal order and on the other hand

28

in that common implicit consent that underlies the possibility of any communication at all.

The point to seize hold of for the purposes of the present investigation is that most forms of contemporary conventionalism have proceeded in such a way as to eliminate habit as an isolable object of inquiry. Some combination of personal and cognitive memory is what the hermeneuticists have standardly been trying to recover and interpret, whereas habitual memory is what they have tended to ignore. I can perhaps best indicate what I mean by this with references to two particular texts. They are Winch's *The Idea of a Social Science* and Sahlins' essay 'La Pensée Bourgeoise: the American Clothing System'. A considerable number of other texts could of course have been chosen instead; I choose these two because they are culturally symptomatic. The approaches they exemplify may be taken as representative of styles of thinking that have been widely adopted in modern social and cultural theory.

The explicit elimination of the notion of habit is evident in that approach to social theory which views particular instances of behaviour as the application of social rules. It is well known that Winch takes his point of departure in *The Idea of a Social Science*[40] from John Stuart Mill's contention that social science might be modelled on natural science. What is less often remarked, but more pertinent to the present discussion, is that in the course of his argument Winch pointedly takes issue with Oakeshott's distinction between two forms of morality.[41] Oakeshott distinguishes between a type of morality which is 'a reflective application of a moral criterion' and a type of morality which is 'a habit of affection and behaviour'.[42] The first form, the reflective application of a moral criterion, may appear as 'the self-conscious pursuit of moral ideals, or as 'the reflective observance of moral rules'; in either case, it is a form of moral life in which a special value is attributed to self-consciousness, whether individual or social. Not only is the rule or the ideal the product of reflective thought, but the application of the rule or ideal to any particular situation is also a reflective activity. This form of moral life therefore entails a particular type of training. It requires a training in the appreciation of moral ideals themselves, a training 'in which the ideals are separated and detached from the necessarily imperfect expression they find in particular actions'; and it requires a training 'in the application of ideals to concrete situations', and in the art of selecting 'appropriate means for achieving the ends which our education has inculcated'.

Oakeshott contrasts this with that form of moral life which he calls 'a habit of affection and conduct'. In this type of moral life everyday situations are said to be met not by 'conduct recognized as the expression of a moral ideal' nor by 'consciously applying to ourselves a rule of behaviour', but by 'acting in accordance with a certain habit of behaviour'. Such a form of moral life does not issue from the consciousness of possible alternative ways of behaving and from a choice, determined by an ideal or a rule or an opinion, from among the perceived alternatives; conduct here 'is as nearly as possible without reflection'. Accordingly, in most of the current situations of life there is no weighing up of alternatives and no reflection on the possible consequences of action; on any particular occasion there is 'nothing more than the unreflective following of a tradition of conduct in which we have been brought up'. For these habits of affection and behaviour are not to be learned by precept, but only by 'living with people who habitually behave in a certain manner'. We acquire such habits in the same way that we acquire our native language. Just as there is no point in a child's life at which it can be said to learn the language which is habitually spoken in its hearing, so equally there is no point in its life at which it can be said to begin to learn habits of behaviour from the people constantly about it. Even though, in both cases, what is learned, or at least some of it, can be formulated in rules and precepts, in neither case do we, in this kind of education, 'learn by learning rules and precepts'. What we learn, in acquiring habits of conduct as in acquiring a language, may be learned without the formulation of rules. And indeed, Oakeshott insists, such practical knowledge of rules as this command of language or behaviour entails is impossible until we have forgotten them as rules and are no longer tempted to turn speech and action into the application of rules to a situation. In sum, Oakeshott wants to say that the dividing line between behaviour which is habitual and behaviour which is rule-governed depends upon whether or not a rule is consciously applied; and he insists that a substantial part of human behaviour can be described in terms of the notion of habit, such that neither the idea of a rule nor the idea of reflectiveness is essential to it.

Against this Winch argues that the test of whether a person's actions are the application of a rule is not whether they can formulate the rule but whether it makes sense to distinguish between a right and a wrong way of doing things in connection with what they do. And where that makes sense, 'it must also make sense to say that he is applying a criterion in what he does even though he does not, and perhaps cannot, formulate that criterion'.[43] Winch infers from this that Oakeshott is right to say that learning a form of conduct is like learning to speak a language, but that he draws a false inference from the analogy. Learning to speak a language entails being able to go on speaking sentences that have not been shown one. There is evidently a sense in which this involves doing something different from what I have been shown. Yet in relation to the linguistic rules that I am following this still counts as 'going on in the same way' as I have been shown. And this brings out what is meant here when we speak of going on in the same way. There is a sense in which to acquire a habit is to acquire a propensity to go on doing the same kind of thing; but there is another sense in which this is true of learning a rule. These two senses, Winch emphasises, are different, and much hinges upon the difference.[44] If it were merely a question of habits, he argues, then our current behaviour might certainly be influenced by the way in which we had acted in the past; but that would be just a causal influence. The dog responds to N's commands now in a certain way because of what has happened to the dog in the past. If I am told to continue the series of natural numbers beyond 100, I continue in a certain way because of my past training. The phrase 'because of' is being used differently of these two situations. The dog has been conditioned to respond in a certain way, whereas I know the correct way to proceed on the basis of what I have been taught. Winch wants to say that I can be said to have acquired a rule, rather than a habit, because I understand what is meant by 'doing the same thing on the same kind of occasion'. The notion of a rule of conduct and the notion of meaningful action are interwoven; it is indispensable to our identifying actions as actions – rather than as mere bodily happenings or physiological events – that they be seen as meaningful actions. The most important category for our understanding of social life, then, will not be that of cause and effect but that of meaningfulness. By this move Winch leaves the notion of habit with no significant work to do for social theory.

By making this distinction between habits and rules, Winch is able to argue that those forms of activity which Oakeshott describes as 'habits of affection and conduct' are properly describable as rule-following behaviour. Winch mentions several examples of rule-governed behaviour; I shall cite one example which he does not give but which captures his meaning. A term like 'shame' refers us to a certain type of situation, the shameful, and to a certain manner of response to the situation, that of hiding oneself or of seeking to wipe out the stain. Hiding in this context is intended to cover up the shame; we can understand what is meant by hiding here only if we comprehend what kind of situation and feeling is being talked about. A term like shame, then, can be explained only by reference to a specific language of interaction in which we blame, exhort, admire and esteem each other. In the case of situations judged to be shameful there may be no systematic formulation of the norms and of the conception of men and society which underlie them. But the understanding of these norms and of that conception is nonetheless implicit in our ability to apply the appropriate descriptions to particular actions and situations. These practices require the possibility of certain self-descriptions by the participants and such self-descriptions are constitutive of those practices.[45]

Sahlins arrives at a position analogous to that advanced by Winch but by a different route: that is, by applying the methods of structural linguistics to the 'language' of clothes. In his study of the American clothing system Sahlins dispenses with any notion of habit, not explicitly but by implication.[46] What he is concerned to reject explicitly is the supposition that the social meaning of clothes has any necessary connection with their physical properties. Against this he argues that the social meaning of objects of apparel that makes them useful to certain categories of persons is symbolic and arbitrary. In making this claim, Sahlins deliberately applies the premise of Saussure's distinction between language and speech, which from the outset sets aside what he called the 'physical aspect of communication'.[47] This means that what is important is not how a sound is produced but the way in which it is distinguished from other sounds. The sound p, for example, is studied not as a sound which results from closing the lips and the absence of any vibration of the vocal chords, but as a sound opposed to the series v and f as an occlusive, to the series b, g and d as a voiceless consonant, and to the series t and k as a labial. It thus becomes possible to characterise a language, not with reference to the physiological details of its articulation through the role it imposes on the vocal chords and the soft palate, but with reference to the way in which each sound is distinguished from all other sounds in a system of opposites. This independence of language from the phonetic substratum is the most important element of structuralism: phonology is structural because it is interested in sounds in so far as the various sounds of a language are defined solely by their relation with one another. Having in this way set aside at the outset the physical aspect of communication, Saussure then isolates what he calls the 'executive side'. What is given as intelligible is language as a systematic organisation of potential arrangements on the basis of which a particular speaker produces speech as a particular message. Speech cannot then constitute the unique object of a specific discipline, but is dispersed across different domains. Even if it can be scientifically described, this falls to the task of many sciences, including acoustics, physiology, sociology and the history of semantic changes. Saussure's objectivism is thus unable to conceive of speech, and more generally of practice, other than as execution within a logic which is that of the code to be applied.

Sahlins goes on from these premises to argue that the system of clothing is like the structure of a language. The clothing scheme is 'a kind of general syntax', a 'generative grammar', and a set of 'semantic oppositions'. The scheme operates as a set of rules for declining and combining classes of clothing so as to map the cultural universe. In manufacturing apparel of distinct cut, outline and colour an item of clothing becomes appropriate for men or women, for night or day, for around the house or in public, for adult or adolescent; what is here produced are classes of time and place which index situations and activities, and classes of status to which all persons are ascribed. By deploying binary contrasts between heavy/light, rough/smooth, hard/soft, any piece of cloth becomes a particular combination of textural qualities; what is here produced, again, is a set of propositions concerning age, sex, activity, class, time and place. Thus given rules of combination comparable to a syntax, a clothing system – it is argued – can develop a series of propositions which constitute so many statements about the relations between persons and situations in the cultural system. As a materialisation of the main co-ordinates of person and occasion, clothing becomes a complex scheme of cultural categories and the relations between them; the code is decodable at a glance because it works at an unconscious level, the conception being built into visual perception itself.

It should be noted that the language of clothes is here being described from the standpoint of the perceiver, not the wearer. There can be no doubt of the analytical purchase this gives; nineteenth-century clothing, for example, provides a field-day for a taxonomist in search of binary oppositions. Its garments signalled to the world the role the wearers were expected to play and reminded them of the responsibilities and constraints of their role. The role of men was to be serious (they wore dark colours with little ornamentation), active (their clothes allowed them movement), strong (their clothes emphasised broad chests and shoulders), and aggressive (their clothes had sharp lines and a clearly-defined silhouette). The role of women was to be frivolous (they wore light pastel colours, ribbons, laces and bows), inactive (their clothes inhibited movement), delicate (their clothes accentuated small waists and sloping shoulders), and submissive (their clothes were constricting). But now let us switch the perspective from the perceiver to the wearer. The apparel worn by Victorian women not only conveyed *decodable* messages; it also helped to *mould* female behaviour. Clothes were signs. They also constricted. 'No one but a woman', wrote Mrs Oliphant in 1879, 'knows how her dress twists about her knees, doubles her fatigue, and arrests her locomotive powers.'[48] Tight skirts and sleeves, crinolines and trains, floor-length petticoats – they all arrested her locomotive powers. But no encumbrance was more graphically constricting than the tight-laced corset, worn almost universally in England and America throughout the nineteenth century. Its defenders and its opponents were in agreement about many of its effects. The defenders of tight-lacing spoke of 'discipline', 'submission', 'bondage', and 'confinement'; the epithet 'straight-laced' survives as a memento of a time when wearing a corset was seen as a moral imperative. The opponents of tight-lacing compared the practice with Chinese foot-binding and insisted that it caused deformity; they worried about the compression of vital organs in the soft boneless area of the waist, the displacement of the ribs, and the complaints of general weakness – debility, fatigue, low vitality – that this brought on. Both opponents and defenders of the corset were in a sense in agreement: it was designed to constrict the diaphragm and change the configuration of the body. The effect, in other words, begins to look rather less like Sahlins' 'semantic opposition' and rather more like Oakeshott's 'habits of affection and behaviour'. And this raises the whole question of what we mean by the constitution of social categories, by bringing into the open the double meaning of the term 'constitution'. For the Victorian clothing system did not only signal the existence of categories of behaviour, it also produced the existence of those categories of behaviour and kept them habitually in being by moulding bodily configuration and movement.

There is, then, a striking parallel between the lines of inquiry suggested by Sahlins and by Winch. In each case the idea of *habit* has been eliminated by a strategy of separation. Winch abandons the concept of habit in favour of the idea of a social rule, while Sahlins has no need for a concept of habit in a science of signs whose aim is to decode a structure of grammatical possibilities. Habit is either explicitly abandoned or implicitly ignored. It is explicitly rejected in a form of investigation which separates the rule and its application; and it is implicitly rejected in a mode of inquiry which separates the code and its execution. But it is on the executive side, on the side of application, that a weakness of these models lies. For as soon as one moves attention from the structure of a language to the uses which agents in practice make of it, one sees that mere knowledge of the language, a knowledge of the rule or the code, gives only imperfect mastery of those practices that have been subsumed under the parallel terms of application and execution. In such a picture, whether of a language or of sets of practices understood on the analogy of a language, no place and hence no significance is assigned to that *accumulative practice of the same* in which habitual skill resides. There is, as it were, a gap between the two terms which are here analogously employed: a gap between rule and application, and a gap between code and execution. This gap must, I shall suggest, be reclaimed by a theory of habitual practice, and, therefore, of habit-memory.

The point of insisting upon the fact of this gap is to show that there is something distinguishable as social habit-memory and to put oneself into the position where one can begin to look more closely at how that works. As such, social habits have a quite separate significance from individual habits. It is no more part of my purpose to inquire into the working of distinctively individual habits than it was part of the undertakings of the kind represented by Winch and Sahlins to do that. For an individual habit does not have a meaning for others in the sense that it rests on others' conventional expectations within the context of a system of shared meanings. Of course, a purely individual or personal habit, of greater or lesser triviality, can be interpreted as meaningful by others. An individual may be in the habit of doodling during lectures; and others might interpret that behaviour as meaningful, either in the sense that it can be taken to be unintentionally symptomatic of a person's temperament, or in the sense that it can be taken to be intentionally conveying the fact that the individual's mind is not fully occupied by the ostensible object of everyone's attention. But it does not meet the criterion of a social habit. For the meaning of a social habit rests upon others' conventional expectations such that it must be interpretable as a socially legitimate (or illegitimate) performance. Social habits are essentially legitimating performances. And if habit-memory is inherently performative, then social habit-memory must be distinctively social-performative.

If we pass in review the three types of memory which I have distinguished – personal, cognitive, and habit-memory – we find that each has been studied or might be studied in ways designed to elucidate the nature of a particular type of failure on the part of the subject whose capacity to remember is being investigated, the nature of the failure being peculiar to that particular kind of memory claim which is being made in each case.

Personal memory has been studied by psychoanalysts as part of an investigation of the life history of individuals. A significant memory failure here would entail the subjects' inability to remember the prototype of their present actions in situations where they deliberately but unconsciously put themselves in distressing circumstances and in this way compulsively repeat, or act out, a prior and causally determining experience.

Cognitive memory has been studied by psychologists as part of an investigation of universal mental faculties. A significant memory failure here, whether of a normal or pathological kind, would entail the subjects' inability to adopt a schema or principle of classification, or their misapplication of that schema or classification in particular instances.

But what kind of forgetting would the forgetting of a social habit-memory entail? It is not entirely clear just how most practitioners of contemporary conventionalism would answer that question. Whereas psychoanalysts have been explicitly interested in the ways in which subjects forget prototypical situations in their life history, and whereas psychologists have been explicitly interested in the ways in which subjects forget to employ or misemploy a schema or category, the practitioners of conventionalism have not been explicitly interested in acts of remembering and forgetting as such. But a conventionalist account necessarily implies an account of forgetting, and what has commonly been implied is that we are dealing here with a form of cognitive memory. That is, from the act of applying the rule or code, or from the failure to apply them, we infer that a particular rule or code has been remembered or forgotten. But I want to say that, in addition to this, something further is involved, and that this is a different type of remembering. The habit-memory – more precisely, the social habit-memory – of the subject is not identical with that subject's cognitive memory of rules and codes; nor is it simply an additional or supplementary aspect; it is an essential ingredient in the successful and convincing performance of codes and rules.

6

The one social theorist not only to have acknowledged the importance of social memory but to have devoted sustained and systematic attention to the ways in which memory is socially constructed is Maurice Halbwachs, particularly in his two important works *Les cadres sociaux de la mémoire* and *La mémoire collective*.[49] He there argued that it is through their membership of a social group – particularly kinship, religious and class affiliations – that individuals are able to acquire, to localise and to recall their memories.

We should try the experiment, he suggested, of passing in review the number of memories which we recall or which are evoked for us in the course of a day by our direct or indirect relations with other people. We will then notice that, most commonly, we appeal to our memory in order to reply to questions which others put to us, or which we imagine that they could ask us, and, in order to reply to them, we envisage ourselves as forming part of the same group or groups as they do. Most frequently, if I recall something that is because others incite me to recall it, because their memory comes to the aid of mine and mine finds support in theirs. Every recollection, however personal it may be, even that of events of which we alone were the witnesses, even that of thoughts and sentiments that remain unexpressed, exists in relationship with a whole ensemble of notions which many others possess: with persons, places, dates, words, forms of language, that is to say with the whole material and moral life of the societies of which we are part or of which we have been part.

This applies, he argues, equally to recent and to distant memories. For what binds together recent memories is not the fact that they are contiguous in time but rather the fact that they form part of a whole ensemble of thoughts common to a group, to the groups with which we are in a relationship at present or have been in some connection in the recent past. When we wish to evoke such memories it is enough if we direct our attention to the prevailing interests of the group and follow the course of reflection customary to it. Exactly the same applies when we want to recall more distant memories. To evoke such memories, it is enough, once again, to direct our attention to the recollections which occupy a primary place in the thoughts of the group. There is no difference, in this respect, between recent and distant memories. It is as beside the point to speak of an association by resemblance in the case of distant memories as it is to speak of an association by contiguity in the case of recent memories. For the kind of association that makes possible retention in the memory is not so much one of resemblance or contiguity as rather a community of interests and thoughts. It is not because thoughts are similar that we can evoke them; it is rather because the same group is interested in those memories, and is able to evoke them, that they are assembled together in our minds.

Groups provide individuals with frameworks within which their memories are localised and memories are localised by a kind of mapping. We situate what we recollect within the mental spaces provided by the group. But these mental spaces, Halbwachs insisted, always receive support from and refer back to the material spaces that particular social groups occupy. He cited Comte's remark that our mental equilibrium is, first and foremost, due to the fact that the physical objects with which we are in daily contact change little or not at all, so providing us with an image of permanence and stability; and he went on to show how no collective memory can exist without reference to a socially specific spatial framework. That is to say, our images of social spaces, because of their relative stability, give us the illusion of not changing and of rediscovering the past in the present. We conserve our recollections by referring them to the material milieu that surrounds us. It is to our social spaces – those which we occupy, which we frequently retrace with our steps, where we always have access, which at each moment we are capable of mentally reconstructing – that we must turn our attention, if our memories are to reappear. Our memories are located within the mental and material spaces of the group.

Thus Halbwachs explicitly rejected the separation of the two questions: How does the individual preserve and rediscover memories? And how do societies preserve and rediscover memories? With exemplary lucidity, he demonstrated that the idea of an individual memory, absolutely separate from social memory, is an abstraction almost devoid of meaning. He showed how different social segments, each with a different past, will have different memories attached to the different mental landmarks characteristic of the group in question. And he singles out, as illustrative of his general thesis, the particular cases of memory as it works within kinship groups, within religious groups, and within classes. Yet Halbwachs, even though he makes the idea of collective memory central to his inquiry, does not see that images of the past and recollected knowledge of the past are conveyed and sustained by (more or less) ritual performances.

If we follow the thread of Halbwachs's argument we are inevitably led to the question: given that different groups have different memories which are particular to them, how are these collective memories passed on within the same social group from one generation to the next? Halbwachs does little more than hint at answers to this question, confining himself, for the most part, to suggestions that are at once formulaic and anthropomorphic. Thus he says that 'society tends to eliminate from its memory everything which could separate individuals',[50] or that, at certain moments, 'society is obliged to become attached to new values, that is to say to depend upon other traditions which are in better relation with its needs and present tendencies'.[51] Such formulations, co-existing so incongruously with the particularity and vividness of his many acute perceptions, are evidently derived from certain habits of language and method, in particular from a Durkheimian vocabulary, characterised by the employment, with the epithet 'collective', of terms borrowed from individual psychology. This is no minor blemish or lacuna. For if we are to say that a social group, whose duration exceeds that of the lifespan of any single individual, is able to 'remember' in common, it is not sufficient that the various members who compose that group at any given moment should be able to retain the mental representations relating to the past of the group. It is necessary also that the older members of the group should not neglect to transmit these representations to the younger members of the group. If we want to continue to speak, with Halbwachs, of collective memory, we must acknowledge that much of what is being subsumed under that term refers, quite simply, to facts of communication between individuals. That the members of different social groups do in fact communicate with each other within the group in ways that are characteristic of that particular group can indeed be inferred from what Halbwachs says; but it is a matter of inference, because he leaves us with no explicit sense that social groups are made up of a system, or systems, of communication.

The difficulty may be illustrated with an example which Halbwachs himself cites. In the course of discussing family memory he speaks briefly about the role of grandparents. 'It is', he writes, 'in a fragmentary way, and as it were across the intervals of the present family that they communicate their own memories to the grandchildren.'[52] But how are we to think about these 'intervals'? What the remark demonstrates is an inability to pinpoint the characteristic acts of transfer, and so to contextualise properly the ways in which the memories of grandparents, as a social group, are transmitted to grandchildren, as a social group. This is a failure within the terms of his own inquiry; and because it is also a general failure, it is worth pursuing further.

Marc Bloch has drawn attention to the fact that in ancient rural societies, before the institution of the newspaper, the primary school, and military service, the education of the youngest living generation was generally undertaken by the oldest living generation.[33] In such village societies, because working conditions kept mother and father away almost all day, especially during the summer period, the young children were brought up chiefly by their grandparents; so that it is from the oldest members of the household, at least as much as if not indeed more than from their own parents, that the memory of the group was mediated to them. This process began very early in the life of the child. After the first phase of childhood, dominated by nourishment and the relationship with the mother, the child joined the group of siblings and other children living in the household; and it was from this time on that their education was most frequently supervised by grandmother. Until the introduction of the first machines, it was grandmother who was the mistress of the household, who prepared the meals, and who, alone, was occupied with the children. It was her task to teach the language of the group. When the ancient Greeks called stories 'geroia', when Cicero called them 'fabulae aniles', and when the picture illustrating the *Contes* of Perrault represented an old woman telling a story to a circle of children, they were registering the extent to which the grandmother took charge of the narrative activity of the group. In such a context we should not envisage communication between generations as being conducted, so to speak, in 'Indian file', the children having contact with their ancestors only through the mediation of their parents. Rather, with the moulding of each new mind there is at the same time a backward step, joining the most malleable to the most inflexible mentality, while skipping the generation which might be the sponsor of change. And this way of transmitting memory, Bloch suggests, must surely have contributed to a very substantial extent to the traditionalism inherent in so many peasant societies.[34]

My point in focussing on this particular example is to emphasise the fact that to study the social formation of memory is to study those acts of transfer that make remembering in common possible. I mean to isolate and consider in more detail certain acts of transfer that are to be found in both traditional and modern societies. In doing this I wish to lay stress on particular types of repetition; whereas some dominant trends in contemporary social theory are often criticised on the ground that they do not address, or address inadequately, the fact of social change, I shall seek to highlight the way in which such theories are often defective because they are unable to treat adequately the fact of social persistence. It is to this end that I have singled out, as acts of transfer of crucial importance, commemorative ceremonies and bodily practices. As we have seen, these are by no means the only constituents of communal memory; for the production of informally told narrative histories is both a basic activity for our everyday characterisation of human actions and a feature of all social memory. But I have seized upon commemorative ceremonies and bodily practices in particular because it is the study of these, I want to argue, that leads us to see that images of the past and recollected knowledge of the past are conveyed and sustained by (more or less ritual) performances.

2

Commemorative ceremonies

1

Between the seizure of power in January 1933 and the outbreak of war in September 1939, the subjects of the Third Reich were constantly reminded of the National Socialist Party and its ideology by a series of commemorative ceremonies. The number, the sequence and the performative structure of these festivals rapidly assumed a canonical form and they retained that form until the demise of the Third Reich. The impact of this newly-invented canonic sequence pervaded all spheres of life, the festivals of the Reich being related to the feasts of the Christian calendar in much the same way as the latter had been related to the seasonal celebrations of the pagan era. The calendrical liturgy of the National Socialist Party was regulated and total.[1]

The liturgical year began on 30 January with the anniversary of Hitler's seizure of power in 1933. On that day each year Hitler's speech to the Reichstag, transmitted by radio, presented 'the Nation' with an account of what he had done with the power entrusted to him; the torchlight procession of 30 January 1933 was annually repeated; and the day ended with a ceremony, broadcast by radio from every street corner, at which eighteen-year-olds who had demonstrated qualities of leadership in the Hitler Youth were sworn in as full members of the Party. Every year on 24 February a ceremony exclusively for the 'old guard' commemorated the foundation of the Party, the 'annunciation' of the 'immutable' programme of twenty-five points in the Hofbräuhaus in 1920. 16 March was a national day of mourning, taken over from the Weimar Republic and dedicated to the memory of the dead of the Great War. On the last Sunday of every March fourteen-year-olds joined the Hitler Youth in a rite of passage whose focal point, in precise analogy with the confession of belief in Christ at confirmation, was the swearing of allegiance to the Führer. The Führer's birthday on 20 April was celebrated with a parade of the Wehrmacht

41

through the Brandenburg Gate. The national festival of the German people, held on 1 May, and originating as a workers' festival, was stripped of its internationalist overtones and reinterpreted as a celebration of German *Volksgemeinschaft*. On 21 June the summer solstice was celebrated by parades of the SS and Hitler Youth. In early September the Party demonstrated its power at the Reichsparteitag. From 1927 to 1938 this week-long rally took place at Nuremberg, the attendance averaging half a million and reaching a record 950,000 in 1938. In early October the old custom of the Harvest Festival was turned into a National Socialist Festival of the German peasantry.

No festival was infused with more potent cultic force than that which commemorated the Putsch, the 'blood baptism' of 1923. Its theme was the sacrifice, the struggle, and the eventual victory of the 'old fighters' of National Socialism. The survivors of the Putsch, decorated with their 'Blood Order', met for the traditional gathering in the Munich Bürgerbräu-keller on 8 November, there to listen to Hitler's memorial address dedicated to 'the sixteen martyrs of the National Socialist movement'. On the following day the 'old fighters' marched from the Bürgerbräukeller to the Feldherrnhalle, ritually repeating the march of 1923, along a route marked by burning torches, to the accompaniment of funereal music, the tolling of bells, and the slow recital of the names of all those killed since 1919 in the service of the Party. These ceremonies reached their apogee of pageantry in 1935. In that year, the exhumed corpses of the sixteen 'blood witnesses' were placed in the Feldherrnhalle on the eve of the memorial day, and conveyed on 9 November in solemn procession to the newly-built Ehren-tempel on the Königplatz. The route was marked by two hundred and forty columns, each bearing the name of one of 'the fallen of the movement'. As the head of the procession reached each column the names of one of the dead was called out. As the procession arrived at the Feld-herrnhalle sixteen cannon shots rang out, one for each of the sixteen fallen of 1923. As the coffins were placed on carriages for conveyance to the Ehrentempel, Hitler laid a wreath on the memorial. At the Ehren-tempel the names of the sixteen 'blood witnesses' were called out individually, the chorus of Hitler Youth responded to the intonation of each name with the cry 'Here!' and after each cry three shots rang out in salute. This commemoration was a pagan Passion Play drenched in borrowed religious vocabulary.

The narrative tells of historical events – but of historical events transfig-ured by mythicisation into unchanging and unchangeable substances. The contents of the myth are represented as being not subject to any kind of change. The myth teaches that history is not a play of contingent forces.

The fundamental constants are struggle, sacrifice, victory. The cardinal virtues of National Socialism, made flesh, as it were, in the sixteen 'blood witnesses', are unconditional obedience, absolute trust, preparedness for sacrifice to the point of death. The political fiasco of 1923 is in this way re-interpreted and re-presented as neither a defeat nor meaningless nor futile. The mortal fate of those who fell in it is to be interpreted not as a senseless death but as a sacrificial death. It is to be understood as a sacred event, and one which points forward to another sacred event, that of 30 January 1933. For the seizure of power is interpreted as no more a mere political success than the putsch of 1923 is a mere political failure. Neither belongs to the sphere of mundane things. The 'sacred' event of the putsch prefigured victory, while the 'sacred' event of the seizure of power finally gave real shape to the content of revelation, the 'Reich'. Between the two events a mythic concordance is established. The crucial recurring date of this mythic narrative is 9 November.

This narrative was more than a story told – it was *a cult enacted*. It was a rite fixed and performed. Its story was told not unequivocally in the past tense but in the tense of a metaphysical present. We would underestimate the commemorative hold of the rite, we would minimise its mnemonic power, if we were to say that it *reminded* the participants of mythic events; we should say rather that the sacred event of 1923 was *re-presented*; the participants in the rite gave it ceremonially embodied form. The transfigured reality of the myth was again and again re-presented when those who took part in the cult became so to speak contemporaries with the mythic event. Every year the historical march of 1923 was repeated; every year the sixteen shots rang out, repeating the sixteen deadly shots of 1923; every year the flags were flaunted, not as signs referring back to a finished event but as relics consubstantial with that event. Above all, it was through acts performed at a sacred site that the illusion of mundane time was suspended. It was at the Feldherrnhalle that the mythic structure was every year given present shape. It was at this site that temporal difference was denied and the existence of the same, the 'true' and 'authentic' reality, was annually disclosed.

The National Socialist regime was new and its ceremonies newly invented, even though they deliberately took on some Christian components – of timing and of intrinsic character – in the way in which earlier Christian ceremonies took on some pagan ones. Thus Nazi was to Christian as Christian was to pagan. There is a long-standing German *traditio* – thus identified – and it has been in part kept going performatively.

2

Events of this kind, of course, are part of a broader phenomenon, that of ritual action. There is substantial disagreement as to how the word ritual should be used, but I take it that one of the most succinct and workable definitions on offer is that proposed by Lukes, who suggests that we employ the term ritual to refer to 'rule-governed activity of a symbolic character which draws the attention of its participants to objects of thought and feeling which they hold to be of special significance'.[2] The premises contained in this definition may be unpacked by means of three interconnected propositions, each of which may be most easily stated in a negative form.

Rites are not merely expressive. It is true that they are expressive acts rather than instrumental acts, in the sense that they are either not directed to a strategic end, or if they are so directed, as with fertility rites, they fail to achieve their strategic aim. But rites are expressive acts only by virtue of their conspicuous regularity. They are formalised acts, and tend to be stylised, stereotyped and repetitive. Because they are deliberately stylised, they are not subject to spontaneous variation, or at least are susceptible of variation only within strict limits. They are not performed under inner momentary compulsion but are deliberately observed to denote feelings. They do discharge expressive feelings; but this is not their central point.

Rites are not merely formal. We commonly express our sense of their formalism by speaking of such acts as 'merely' ritual or as 'empty' forms, and we frequently contrast them with acts and utterances which we speak of as 'sincere' or 'authentic'. But this is misleading. For rites are felt by those who observe them to be obligatory, even if not unconditionally so, and the interference with acts that are endowed with ritual value is always felt to be an intolerable injury inflicted by one person or group upon another. We may suppose the beliefs someone else holds sacred to be merely fantastic, but it can never be a light matter to demand that their actual expression be violated. And conversely, people resist being forced to pay lip-service to an alien set of rites, incompatible with their own vision of the 'truth', because to enact a rite is always, in some sense, to assent to its meaning. To make patriots insult their flag or to force pagans to receive baptism is to violate them.

Rites are not limited in their effect to the ritual occasion. It is true that rituals tend to occur at special places at fixed times. And it is the case that many rites mark beginnings and endings, both in individual life-crisis ceremonies – for example those associated with birth, puberty, marriage and death – and in recurrent calendrical ceremonies. But whatever is demonstrated in rites permeates also non-ritual behaviour and mentality.

Although demarcated in time and space, rites are also as it were porous. They are held to be meaningful because rites have significance with respect to a set of further non-ritual actions, to the whole life of a community. Rites have the capacity to give value and meaning to the life of those who perform them.[3]

All rites are repetitive, and repetition automatically implies continuity with the past. But there is a distinctive class of rites which have an explicitly backward-looking and calendrical character. National Socialist festivals are of this kind. It is easy to think of further instances. Thus in many cultures festivals are represented as the commemoration of myths which are attached to them and as recalling an event held to have taken place at some fixed historical date or in some mythical past; there are recurrent calendrical ceremonials such as New Year's Day and birthdays; the festivals of Christian saints are commemorated on certain days of the year; ceremonies of remembrance are held at the Cenotaph; flags are flown at half-mast; flowers are placed on graves; and there are now more than a hundred embassies in all of the major world capitals, each of them with at least one national celebration to which officials must be invited every year. Some of these commemorations are willingly observed, some are a burden, and some provoke no more than a mildly excited yawn. But the feature which they all share, and which sets them apart from the more general category of rites, is that they do not simply imply continuity with the past but explicitly claim such continuity. And many of them, on which I now wish to fasten attention, do so by ritually re-enacting a narrative of events held to have taken place at some past time, in a manner sufficiently elaborate to contain the performance of more or less invariant sequences of formal acts and utterances.

Nowhere is this explicit claim to be commemorating an earlier set of founding events in the form of a rite more abundantly expressed than in the great world religions; this claim appears there again and again.

The core of the Jewish identity is established by reference to a sequence of historical events. The two most popular books in Jewish life, the Old Testament and the Jewish prayer-book, narrate and celebrate this sequence. The Old Testament, and particularly its historical books, disclose an identity formed by the phases of a historical narrative: the career of Abraham and his migration to Egypt, the exodus of the Jewish tribes from Egypt, the revelation of the Law on Mount Sinai, the entry of the Jews into the Promised Land, and their subsequent adventures under the judges and the kings. The prayer-book, like the Old Testament, both expresses the religious-ethical ideals of Judaism and reflects the life of the Jew as a member of a particular historic group; while its basic elements remain identical throughout the Diaspora, in almost every country the details of the prayer-book bear the impress of the local conditions to which the Jewish community in the country in question was subjected. In both the Old Testament and the prayer-book 'remembrance' becomes a technical term through which expression is given to the process by which practising Jews recall and recuperate in their present life the major formative events in the history of their community. Nowhere is this theology of memory more pronounced than in Deuteronomy. For the Deuteronomist the test of showing that the new generation of Israel remains linked to the tradition of Moses, that present Israel has not been severed from its redemptive history, is to be met by a form of life in which to remember is to make the past actual, to form a solidarity with the fathers. This test is to be met in cultic demonstration; Israel observes festivals in order to remember. What is remembered is the historical narrative of a community. Of the major festivals in the Jewish year, Passover is explicitly historical, reminding the people every year of the central event of ancient Jewish history, the Exodus from Egypt as told in Exodus 12. Seder annually reminds practising Jews of the most formative moment in the life of their community, the moment in which that community was redeemed from bondage and made into a free people, and it reminds them of that moment in the form of a home celebration, in which a prominent part in the service is assigned to the child. The generations in history hang together cultically. Then too, the harvest festivals of Shevuoth and Sukkoth have been given historical reference: the first commemorating the revelation of the Law on Mount Sinai, the second alluding to the Exodus. Two minor festivals are explicitly historical, keeping in mind events remembered annually: Purim, commemorating the events related in the Book of Esther, and Hanukka, celebrating the story of the purification of the Temple. Even the Sabbath is presented in the Pentateuch in partly historical terms, as a commemoration of both the creation of the world and the Exodus; by keeping the Sabbath holy, Israel remembers and participates in the redemptive history of its community.[4]

Christianity stands or falls with the tie that binds it to its unique historical origin. It originates at a definite historical moment and at all subsequent points in its history it explicitly and elaborately refers back to that moment. Christianity begins with a single sequence of events in history and above all with the central event of the crucifixion. About the historicity of the crucifixion and about the date on which it occurred there can be no serious doubt. Christianity is thus neither the exposition of an abstract doctrine nor the recapitulation of a myth. It teaches that divine revelation has assumed a historical form, that God has intervened in the history of humanity, and that the vocation of the Christian is to remember and commemorate the history of that intervention. The period of time evoked

46

by the Gospels and recalled in the liturgy is not, as in archaic religions, a mythical time, and the events annually recapitulated in the sacred calendar are not to be thought of as events that occurred 'in the beginning', 'in illo tempore'. The events took place in a datable history and at a clearly-defined historical period, the period in which Pontius Pilate was governor in Judaea. Those events and that period are commemorated annually in the Good Friday and Easter festivals. The whole Christian year is articulated around this paschal period which recapitulates and re-enacts, in the sequence of the ceremonies and the content of the prayers, the various phases of the Passion. Enclosed within this annual cycle there is a weekly periodicity, for on each Sunday the Mass in which the faithful participate commemorates the Last Supper. But indeed there is no prayer and no act of devotion which does not refer back, whether directly or indirectly, to the historical Christ; the historical narrative reaches the minutest particulars. The fact of the crucifixion is symbolised in each sign of the cross: itself a condensed commemoration, a narrative made flesh, an evocation of the central historical fact and the central religious belief of Christianity.[5]

The establishment of Islam as a religion is an even more explicitly defined sequence of historical events than is the case with either Judaism or Christianity: the founder of Islam became a sovereign in his lifetime, governed a community and commanded armies. It is true that important motivations for the growth of a historically referential ritual, present in Judaism and Christianity, were absent in Islam. The life of Muhammad lacked symbolic ambiguity, the hermeneutic incitement in which, as in the Last Supper or the Exodus, the two levels of religious and mundane existence, of sacred and profane time, appear to merge and to call for ritual re-enactment by subsequent believers. The history of the Arab community could not be drawn upon as a rich vein of events or stages of development deserving religious commemoration, since an organised Muslim community quickly sprang into being within a decade after Muhammad had begun to preach. And the absence of a priestly class restricted the development of Islamic liturgy in range and in detail, and meant that the outward manifestations of Islamic religion retained a dominant note of simplicity. In consequence, the Islamic calendar originally contained only two festivals: the Pilgrimage, with the feast celebrating its successful conclusion; and Fasting in Ramadan, with the feast marking the end of the period of abstention. But both festivals have at least some ostensible historical reference. The annual pilgrimage to Mecca has some historical allusion; it evokes the memory of Muhammad, as well as that of Abraham who is credited in the Koran with having founded the sanctuary and instituted the pilgrimage. Every Muslim is enjoined to make the journey to these holy places once in a lifetime, to take part in ceremonial actions at a given time and in a given sequence. Yet although the canon lawyers have devoted much attention to defining the 'ability' to make the Pilgrimage and the conditions which exempt the believer from the obligation to undertake it, in practice the decision whether or not to journey to Mecca is left more or less to the individual, and at no period could more than a small fraction of the Muslim community have taken part. But while the obligation to make the Pilgrimage can have been actually fulfilled only by a small number of Muslims, the obligation of fasting through the month of Ramadan profoundly influences the life of every believer; the fasting has come to be viewed by many as the most important religious act and is observed even by Muslims who may neglect their daily prayers. And Ramadan was selected because of its explicit historic references; it was in this month, the fifth of the Muslim year, that the Koran was sent down as guidance for the people.[6]

3

Thus in the world religions, but also in the rites of many preliterate peoples and in a number of modern political rituals too, there exist a variety of ceremonies which share certain common features: they do not simply imply continuity with the past by virtue of their high degree of formality and fixity; rather, they have as one of their defining features the explicit claim to be commemorating such a continuity. May we not then infer from this that such commemorative ceremonies play a significant role in the shaping of communal memory? Scepticism has frequently been expressed about this inference, and that scepticism has commonly assumed one of three possible forms.

The first line of argument, which I shall call the psychoanalytic position, consists in the view that ritual behaviour is best understood as a form of symbolic representation. Rites are said to be the systematically indirect statement, encoded in the symbolism of the rite, of conflicts which that rite disguises and to that extent denies. The primary process, which is held to explain the secondary process of symbolic representation, is located in the life-history of the individual, although particular psychoanalytic interpretations of ritual may vary according as to whether the oedipal phase or the pre-oedipal phase of childhood or some other conflictual process is seized upon as the genesis of such representations. What all such interpretations have in common is that they decode the ritual text as conflict-laden and hence as in some way freighted with strategies of denial.

It is possible to interpret rituals psychoanalytically as symbolic representations by explaining such representations in terms of the life-history of the individual. Thus Freud's understanding of ritual is based on the supposed analogy between ontogenesis and phylogenesis, the ground for the alleged analogy being provided by his view that the oedipal struggle between sons and fathers in the context of patriarchal authority is the primary process.[7] On this basis Freud is led to speculate that in the life-history of the human race there once existed a primal horde consisting of a powerful father, his sons, and a group of females to whom the father had exclusive access; that the sons, resenting his dominance, killed him; that subsequently they recognised that they loved as well as hated him, and were overcome with remorse; and that, in reparation, they restored the image of the father in the substitutive form of the totemic animal. On this interpretation, their annually repeated totemic meal should then be seen as the solemn repetition, not of the act of parricide itself, but of the view of that act which those who had committed it subsequently came to take. It was a return of the repressed memory in which they both acted out and overcame the originating act. They acted out their ambivalence toward the father, by simultaneously worshipping and devouring the totemic animal; and they overcame their ambivalence toward the father, by identifying with the animal they ate. The totemic meal is to be understood as an act of symbolic representation in the sense that it was a repetition and a commemoration of this memorable and criminal deed. Without requiring us to swallow the Freudian ontology whole, or to accept its projection onto the life-history of humanity, Richard Wollheim proposes an alternative psychoanalytic explanation of ritual as coded representation.[8] Beginning with the observation that many rites require a death, generally that of an animal, although sometimes the death or simulated death of a human being, he suggests that such acts are invariably 'exercises in denial' and as such belong to the 'pathology of ritual'. The ritual denies, and those who perform it deny, the fact of aggression as a human motive. The denial is accomplished by 'bracketing'. The end to which aggression as a motive inherently moves, the taking of a life, is isolated; once isolated, this end is prescribed, as something which should be repeated over and over again, but always, at each repetition, the life is to be taken out of a motive as far removed from aggression as possible – out of piety or decency or reverence for authority. What such rites are designed to achieve, he suggests, is 'the belittlement or making light of sadism'; and this end can be accomplished only, just as rites in Freud's alternative scenario can be achieved, by encoded quasi-textual representation.

A second line of argument, which I shall call the sociological position, consists in the view that ritual behaviour is best understood as a form of quasi-textual representation. This type of reading then goes on to emphasise the ways in which ritual functions to communicate shared values within a group and to reduce internal dissension; what rituals tell us, on this view, is how social stability and equilibrium are constituted. They show us what a culture's ethos and the sensibility shaped by that ethos look like when spelled out externally, articulated in the symbolism of something like a single collective text.

Many influential variants of this line of interpretation are available. Thus one may, with Durkheim, see ritual as 'representing' social reality by making it intelligible, even if the cognitive content of the rite must be encoded in a metaphorical and symbolic form; and one may thus view religious rituals, for example, as systems of ideas in which 'the individuals represent to themselves the society of which they are members, and the obscure but intimate relations which they have with it'.[9] This idea, derived from highlighting the strongly cognitive aspect to Durkheim's account, that rites may be interpreted as symbolic representations, and in this sense as possessing cognitive content, can be both extended and modified. It can be extended once we interpret the symbolism of political rituals as representing particular concepts of what a society is and of how it functions.[10] And it can be modified once we interpret such political rituals as operating within political contexts in which power is distributed in a systematically unequal way, so that rituals may be understood as exercising cognitive control by providing the official version of the political structure with symbolic representations of, for example, 'the Empire' or 'the Constitution' or 'the Republic' or 'the Nation'.[11] Such rituals are readable as a kind of symbolic collective text. But the possibility of interpreting rites as forms of symbolic representation may be pressed even further still if, with Bakhtin, we read carnival, and more particularly the popular festivities that flourished during the Renaissance, as anticipative representations.[12] For here the inversions of hierarchic order characteristic of carnival are to be read no longer as a covert means of reaffirming hierarchy, but, on the contrary, as a mechanism of social liberation in which the device of symbolic representation is employed as leverage. Carnival is here seen as an act in which 'the people' organise themselves 'in their own way' as a collectivity in which the individual members become an inseparable part of the human mass, such that 'the people' become aware of their sensual-material bodily unity. By enabling such a collective body to coalesce, popular-festive forms may then be said to provide the people with a symbolic representation not of present categories but of utopia, the image of a future state in which there occurs the 'victory of all the people's material abundance, freedom, equality, brotherhood'. The rites of the carnival represent and foreshadow the rights of the people. As a way of interpreting rites, this offers us a different species of symbolic encoding, one in which the otherwise unsaid and unsayable is expressed and the dimension of future time is implicitly laid open; but as an interpretation of ritual action, nonetheless, it belongs within the same genus as its Durkheimian counterpart, that of symbolic representation in a kind of collective text.

A third line of argument, which I shall call the historical position, consists in the view that rites cannot be satisfactorily understood in terms of their internal structure alone. For all rituals, no matter how venerable the ancestry claimed for them, have to be invented at some point, and over the historical span in which they remain in existence they are susceptible to a change in their meaning. This thought has prompted the attempt to rediscover the meaning of ceremonials by resituating them in their historical context. On this view, to set a rite in its context is seen not as an auxiliary step but as an essential ingredient to the act of interpreting it; to investigate the context of a rite is not just to study additional information about it, but to put ourselves in a position to have a greater understanding of its meaning than would be accessible to someone who read it as a self-contained symbolic text.[13] Pursuing this line of thought, many historians have demonstrated that if we are to rediscover the meaning of royal rituals in the early modern period we have to relate them comprehensively to the circumstances in which they were performed.[14] And many other historians, specialising in a later period, have shown that whenever the social institutions for which 'old' traditions were designed begin to crumble under the impact of rapid social change, a widespread and instant invention of new rituals occurs.[15] The invention of ritual turns out to be both a general problem and a phenomenon of particular interest in post-traditional societies.

Thus it is now abundantly clear that in the modern period national élites have invented rituals that claim continuity with an appropriate historic past, organising ceremonies, parades and mass gatherings, and constructing new ritual spaces. This is as true of Europe as of the Middle East. Both the Third Republic and Wilhelmine Germany invested symbolic capital in invented traditions.[16] In France Bastille Day became a historic date in 1880 and in Germany the Franco-Prussian War became a historic event on its twenty-fifth anniversary when a commemorative ceremony was instituted in 1896. Both commemorated the founding acts of the new regime, differing only in the way the foundation myth was interpreted. In both cases the context of the rites demonstrates their ideological function. In France the moderate Republican bourgeoisie invented a rite as part of their strategy for warding off the threat of political enemies on the left; this they achieved by an annual reassertion of France as the nation of 1789 in which the symbols of the tricolour and Marseillaise and the reference to Liberty, Equality, Fraternity, reminded the citizens of the Third Republic of the allegedly unifying fact of French nationhood. In Germany the regime of

Wilhelm II invented ceremonies as part of their strategy for assuring a people who had no political definition before 1871 that they did indeed enjoy a national identity; this they accomplished by celebrating the Bismarckian unification of Germany as the one national historical experience shared by all the citizens of the new empire. In more recent times two celebrations in the Middle East have ritually reinvented ancient history.[17] One was the commemoration of the heroic defence and fall of Masada in the Jewish revolt against the Romans in AD 66; the other was a celebration, inaugurated by the Shah of Iran, of the 2,500th anniversary of the foundation of the Persian state and monarchy by Cyrus the Great. Both cults, that of Masada and that of Cyrus, refer to themes long forgotten and indeed unknown among their respective peoples, the Rabbinic tradition knowing nothing of Masada, the Persians preserving no record of Cyrus. In both cases the memory was recovered from outside sources, received political sponsorship, and was made the focus of national festivities. In Israel the bones found in the ruins of Masada were solemnly reinterred with a military ceremony; in Iran ceremonies were organised at the tomb of Cyrus. The cult of Masada was designed to restore the submerged political-military aspect of Jewish identity; the cult of Cyrus was designed to dramatise the transformation of the Persians from a religious community with an identity focussed on Islam to a secular nation with an identity focussed on Iran. Both sets of invented rites celebrated national heroism.

The types of explanation which I have just passed in review, and which for the sake of clarity I have called the psychological, sociological and historical explanation of ritual action, all proceed by seeking to get behind the ostensible purpose and meaning of rites in order to get at the 'real' purpose and meaning which is said to lie behind their surface. And this gives rise to the question as to whether we can have good reason to think that rituals which are represented as being explicitly commemorative do indeed have the significance, as means of transmitting social memory, which is claimed for them by their participants. That question can best be addressed, I suggest, in two stages: by considering first those features of ritual form which commemorative ceremonies share with other ritual acts of an extended and elaborated kind; and by considering then those features which mark off commemorative ceremonies as rituals of a distinctive kind.

I want to argue that in seeking to understand those features which commemorative ceremonies share with other elaborate rituals, we are liable to be impeded by a tendency, characteristic of most modern interpretations of ritual, to focus attention on the content rather than on the *form* of ritual. And I want then to argue that in seeking to understand those features which distinguish commemorative ceremonies as rituals of a particular kind, we are liable to be impeded by a tendency, characteristic of much modern self-interpretation, to devalue or ignore the pervasiveness and importance in many cultures of actions which explicitly take place as a *re-enactment* of other actions that are considered prototypical. Our understanding of commemorative ceremonies thus encounters obstacles on two counts.

4

I turn now to the first difficulty: the tendency to focus attention on the content rather than on the form of ritual. All three methods of interpreting ritual which I have just reviewed share a common assumption. All explain ritual as a form of symbolic representation. All seek to understand the hidden 'point' that lies 'behind' ritual symbolism by an act of translation in which the encoded text of the ritual is decoded into another language. To fasten upon the hidden symbolic content of ritual is to train attention on those of its features which it shares with certain other ways of articulating meaning in a structured form, particularly myths and dreams. Yet this emphasis on shared features in all three positions, though often illuminating, by definition cannot tell us anything about the identifying features of ritual. I return to this topic later. Let us, beforehand, first look at the evident analogy with myth, and then at the ways in which myth and ritual diverge.

Both ritual and myth may quite properly be viewed as collective symbolic texts; and on this basis one may then go on to suggest that ritual actions should be interpreted as exemplifying the kind of cultural values that often also are expressed in the elaborate statements that we call myths – as exemplifying these values in another medium. Thus Lévi-Strauss has shown how a group of South American Indian myths constantly refer to a contrast between raw meat and cooked meat on the one hand, and to a contrast between fresh vegetables and putrid vegetables on the other. Raw meat, cooked meat, fresh vegetables and putrid vegetables are all concrete things; but when placed together in a pattern, as these are in many South American Indian myths, this limited number of categories can be made to yield the abstract idea of a contrast between a cultural mode of transformation and a natural mode of transformation. Elaborating on this thought, Edmund Leach remarks that this patterning around the opposition between a cultural process and a natural process can be expressed in different media. For it can be expressed either in words – raw, cooked, fresh, putrid – and displayed in the form of a mythic narrative; or it can be expressed in things, and exhibited through the ritual arrangement of the appropriate objects. The patterning of a ritual or that of a myth can equally serve as a complex store of information.[18]

The problem arises when this point is over-generalised. The example just cited does indeed seem to lead on naturally to the suggestion that ritual actions should be interpreted as exemplifying the type of cultural values that also frequently are expressed in mythic statements, as exemplifying those values in another medium. But a good deal hangs on the phase 'in another medium'. To interpret ritual as an alternative symbolic medium for expressing what may be expressed in other ways, and in particular in the form of myth, is to ignore what is distinctive about ritual itself. Yet once we begin to consider the form of ritual, as distinct from the form of myth, we come to see that ritual is not only an alternative way of expressing certain beliefs, but that certain things can be expressed only in ritual.

Ritual and myth will then be seen to differ structurally in at least one major respect. A myth can be narrated by a singer to an audience as entertainment, or by a parent to children as a lesson, or by a structuralist to implied readers as a set of oppositions. To recite a myth is not necessarily to accept it. What the telling of a myth does not do, and what the performance of a ritual essentially does do, is to specify the relationship that obtains between the performers of the ritual and what it is that they are performing. It follows from this that there is an element of invariance encoded into the structure of ritual that is not present in myth.[19]

This structural difference is evident in the way in which some of the primary myths of Western culture have been reshaped and reinterpreted. The reworkings of myth in dramatic form and the possible limits set to such an enterprise became the object of lively debate in the last decades of the nineteenth century. At that time the view was often expressed that the material which provided the subject matter of great dramatic or tragic works would be treated in a variety of ways until eventually some great dramatist found the complete and definitive form for that material, at which point that particular mythic material was exhausted. Thus it was argued that there had been many dramatic reworkings of the Don Juan myth until it was given perfect embodiment in Mozart's opera; and the same judgement was applied to earlier dramatic versions of the Faust myth until it received definitive form in Goethe's Faust. Hence, so the argument ran, it was pointless to want to produce still another Don Juan after Mozart or still another Faust after Goethe. The point of such arguments was to demonstrate that the creative restructuring of mythic material was a finite process; but this point could not be made without acknowledging the extent to which in each case that process did indeed constitute a history of reinterpretations, a process of substantial and varied reworkings until a definitive shape had been given to the mythic material.

It is possible to envisage a significant creative variance which goes beyond even this and no longer fits a schema in which a prehistory of interpretations is finally superseded by a definitive interpretation. In the case of both the Don Juan myth and the Faust myth it may be appropriate to speak of solutions to the task of reworking the mythic material that were imperfect and preparatory, and of a solution that comes later and is definitive. But the myth of Orestes–Electra cannot be accommodated by such a pattern; here the same mythic material and the same basic tragic situation are dramatically restructured by all three of the great Greek tragedians and then again in a modern form, in *Hamlet*, by the greatest of all modern dramatists. Here are several dramatic representations of the same mythic material which are quite different from one another; even if we leave aside Euripides' version, the authoritative status of which has been disputed by some critics, including Aristotle, there remain three dramas which belong to the greatest of all tragedies but among which it is impossible to pick out any single one and to claim that this, in comparison with the others, represents the definitive reworking of the mythic material.

Thus the dramatic reworking of the myth by Aeschylus and Sophocles generates from the same material fundamentally different meanings. Aeschylus presses the tragic element of the conflict contained in the myth to its extreme by showing the act of matricide as necessary and horrifying in equal measure. In this he diverges from earlier poetic treatments of the myth by Simonides, Stesichoros and Pindar; there, the murder of a mother at the command of a god was represented as a heroic act, or at least the obligation of the son to exact retribution on his mother received much greater emphasis than did the horror of his matricide. Aeschylus brings us to see the horror of the act. Orestes is represented as trapped within the logic of a retributive social order whose workings necessarily entail such obligations as are visited upon him; the declaration of his innocence in the final part of the trilogy is made possible only through the establishment of a court of justice publicly acknowledged as competent to pass verdict whenever disputes over retribution should arise, and acknowledged, therefore, as constituting a form of order whose logic supersedes the workings of the system of blood retribution. But equally, Aeschylus represents the matricide perpetrated by Orestes as fully necessary within the context in which it had to be executed. In his reworking of the myth everything is done to show that Orestes' matricide is objectively necessary and everything combines in this sense to drive him on to the act: the command of the god and the threats of what will follow should that command be ignored; Orestes' awareness, as the legitimate heir, of the condition in which his realm stands; the urgings of the chorus, who incite brother and sister to exact retribution when they waver; the behaviour of

Clytemnestra, who seeks to elude the logic of retribution; and the children's lively memory of the dishonour inflicted upon their father by his wife and murderer. Aeschylus reshapes the myth so as to represent the act of matricide as at once necessary and horrific.

The element of horrific necessity is removed from Sophocles' version. Whereas in Aeschylus the order to exact retribution is initiated by a god and accompanied with threats if not performed, in Sophocles' drama Orestes tells how he travelled to Delphi in order to enquire of the oracle how he should avenge his father's death; the god's directions as to how the act should be accomplished are a response to Orestes' own question, and that question already presupposes his decision to execute the deed. Whereas in Aeschylus Electra early discovers traces of the returned brother's presence, the mutual recognition of brother and sister follows shortly after, and subsequently the two plan and act together, in Sophocles most of the dramatic action has unfolded by the time Orestes returns from exile; the drama focusses largely upon Electra. For most of the action she is inwardly alone. She has received no divine command to exact retribution on her mother. She has begun to doubt whether her brother will return from exile and knows nothing of Apollo's direction to him. She is advised by the Chorus that it is pointless to seek to take action against those who now hold power in the land, that her complaints are of no avail to her father and can only do herself harm. She is advised too by her sister Chrysothemis to let the matter of retribution drop and accommodate herself to circumstances in which the possibility of effective rebellion no longer exists. All the considerations which in Aeschylus drive the protagonists to accomplish retribution are removed from Sophocles' drama. One motivation alone remains. The fact that all other participants in the action have adapted to circumstances and, at least externally, have made their peace with those who now hold power; the fact that no one else feels, as she does, the overwhelming sense of pollution; the fact that she too, could she bring herself to do so, has the option of accommodating to circumstances – it is this that causes her, and her alone, to find her existence spiritually intolerable. Instead of the Aeschylean accumulation of pressing objective considerations, Sophocles singles out the motivation that impels the one exception, that agent who feels more intensely than all the others.

These reshapings of mythic material disclose in an extreme form a feature intrinsic to myth as such. The symbolic content of Greek myth is not exhausted in any single formal arrangement. The symbolic material of such myths does not have the invariance and inertia of something already presignified and formalised. On the contrary, it constitutes something more like *a reservoir of meanings* which is available for possible use again in other structures. The mythic material contains a range of potential meanings significantly in excess of their use and function in any particular arrangement, any single dramatic structure. As is also the case with much of the material in the Old Testament, for instance, although there more in the form of narrative reprise and commentary, a network of mythic events enjoys a significant historicity, a long interpretative process of renewal and variation. The re-use of Greek myths, both within the culture of ancient Greece and beyond that cultural domain, depends upon what may be called a surplus of meaning – a surplus which can be realised in variable interpretative arrangements when the mythic material is restructured in other dramatic forms.[20]

By comparison with myths, the structure of rituals has significantly less potential for *variance*. All rituals, it is true, have to be invented at some point and the details of their articulation may develop or vary in content and significance over the course of time. None the less, there remains a potential for invariance that is built into rites, but not into myths, by virtue of the fact that it is intrinsic to the nature of rituals – but not of myths – that they specify the relationship that obtains between the performance of ritual and what it is that the participants are performing. It follows that if considerable precautions are to be taken to assure the identity of a culture's symbolic material, it will be advisable to direct those precautions to ensuring the identity of its ritual. And indeed many traditional societies in which symbolism appears to be immutable act as though they had seen the risk of too rapid an evolution: they do everything to impede its change. Two traditions in particular give widely documented and impressive evidence of this fact. The liturgy of the Mass has persisted for nearly two millennia, during which time it has changed only very slowly; the creeds recited in the Mass are in their present form very ancient.[21] Again, although some aspects of their liturgies vary considerably, perhaps in this responding to differences of historical circumstance, the rituals of the Ashkenazic Jews of Northern Europe, the Sephardi of the Mediterranean, the Falasha of Ethiopia, the Beni of India, and the Karaites of the Crimea, all retain the dedication of faith called the Shema in a central position.[22]

This endowment with invariance results from the particular way in which liturgical language works. We can characterise this feature negatively, by saying that it does not employ forms of communication which have propositional force. It does not consist in the reporting of events or the description of objects or the statement of experimental findings or the formulation of hypotheses. We can characterise this positively, by saying that liturgical language is a certain form of action and puts something into practice. It is not a verbal commentary on an action external to itself; in and of itself liturgical language is an action. And the nature of this action may be broken down into two distinctive properties, whose existence and

57

effectiveness explains, at the same time, why it is that ritual language works so powerfully as a mnemonic device.[23]

For one thing, ritual is a performative language. A performative utterance does not provide a description of a certain action. The utterance of the performative itself constitutes an action of some kind, beyond the obviously necessary action of producing meaningful sounds; and the action, for instance a promise or a vow, is one that can be performed only by the utterance of certain prescribed words. A liturgy is an ordering of speech acts which occur when, and only when, these utterances are performed; if there is no performance there is no ritual.

For another thing, ritual is a formalised language. Its utterances tend to be stylised and stereotyped and to be composed of more or less invariant sequences of speech acts. The utterances are not produced by the performers but are already encoded in a canon and therefore exactly repeatable. What is referred to in canonical utterance is referred to in sequences of words and acts which have, by definition, been performed before.

The *performativeness* of ritual is partly a matter of utterance: the recurrent utterance of certain characteristic verbs and personal pronouns.[24] Among the verbal utterances most commonly encountered in rites are curses, blessings and oaths; much, if not indeed everything, is thought to depend in each case on the exactitude of the utterance itself.[25] A curse seeks to bring its object under the sway of its power; once pronounced a curse continues to consign its object to the fate it has summoned up and is thought to continue in effect until its potency is exhausted. A blessing is no mere pious wish; it is understood to allocate fortune's gifts by the employment of words. And like the curse and the blessing, the oath is an automatically effective power-word which, if the accompanying assertion cannot be confirmed, dedicates the swearer to this power; testimony on oath is considered decisive as to guilt or innocence. Curses, blessings and oaths, together with other verbs frequently found in ritual language, as for instance 'to ask' or 'to pray' or 'to give thanks', presuppose certain attitudes – of trust and veneration, of submission, contrition and gratitude – which come into effect at the moment when, by virtue of the enunciation of the sentence, the corresponding act takes place. Or better: that act takes place in and through the enunciation. Such verbs do not describe or indicate the existence of attitudes: they effectively bring those attitudes into existence by virtue of the illocutionary act. The same effect is accomplished in ritual language by a characteristic use of personal pronouns. Liturgical language makes special use of 'us' and 'those'; the plural form, in 'we' and 'us', indicates that there are a number of speakers but that they are acting collectively, as if they were only one speaker, a kind of corporate personality. Prior to such pronominal utterance there exists an undifferentiated preparedness, expressed by the presence of all the participants in the place where the liturgy is to be celebrated. Through the utterance of the 'we' a basic disposition is given definitive form, is constituted, among the members of the liturgical community. The community is initiated when pronouns of solidarity are repeatedly pronounced. In pronouncing the 'we' the participants meet not only in an externally definable space but in a kind of ideal space determined by their speech acts. Their speech does not describe what such a community might look like, nor does it express a community constituted before and apart from it; performative utterances are as it were the place in which the community is constituted and recalls to itself the fact of its constitution.

Performatives are encoded also in set postures, gestures and move-ments. The resources of this encoding are elementary. In rites the body is given the appropriate pose and moves through the prescribed actions. The body is held braced and attentive in standing; the hands are folded and placed as though bound in praying; persons bow down and express their impotence by kneeling; or they may completely abandon the upright posture in the abasement of bodily prostration. The relative sparseness of such repertoires is their source of strength. The resources of ordinary language, its semantic range and flexibility of tone and register, the possi-bility of producing statements that can be qualified, ironised and retracted, the conditional and subjunctive tense of verbs, language's capacity to lie, to conceal, and to give ideational expression to that which is not present – all these resources constitute, from one vantage point, a communicative defect. The subtlety of ordinary language is such that it can suggest or imply finely-graded degrees of subordination, respect, disregard and con-tempt. Social interactions can be negotiated through a linguistic element of ambiguity, indeterminacy and uncertainty. But the limited resources of ritual posture, gesture and movement strip communication clean of many hermeneutic puzzles. One kneels or one does not kneel, one executes the movement necessary to perform the Nazi salute or one does not. To kneel in subordination is not to state subordination, nor is it just to communicate a message of submission. To kneel in subordination is to display it through the visible, present substance of one's body. Kneelers identify the disposi-tion of their body with their disposition of subordination. Such perform-ative doings are particularly effective, because unequivocal and materially substantial, ways of 'saying'; and the elementariness of the repertoire from which such 'sayings' are drawn makes possible at once their performative power and their effectiveness as mnemonic systems.[26]

The *formalism* of ritual language has an even more evident mnemonic effect. We can speak of a language as formalised when it is systematically composed so as to restrict the range of available linguistic choices. This is pre-eminently the case with ritual where many linguistic options have been abandoned so that choice of words, syntax and style is markedly more restricted than in everyday language. The economy of formalisation is not, of course, exclusive to ritual; the device of 'canonical parallelism', which figures largely in ritual speech, is found too in traditional oral poetry. A tradition of canonical parallelism may be said to exist, according to Jakobson, 'where certain similarities between successive verbal sequences are compulsory or enjoy a high preference'; hence the recurrence of a standardised body of 'conventionally fixed pairs of words'.[27] A vast corpus of research has demonstrated the prominence of such linguistic parallelism throughout the world's oral literatures and its importance there as a mnemonic device.[28] The classic case is that of Finnish oral poetry, the epic deeds recorded in the *Kalevala* being the most frequently cited example of parallel poetry after that of the Old Testament; Bloomfield has argued that the 'catenary structure' of Vedic texts is also 'analogous to so-called parallelism in Hebrew poetry';[29] traditions of parallelism have been documented too for ancient Chinese and early Greek, for numerous 'folk' traditions in South India and Southeast Asia, and among American Indian languages, most notably in ancient Maya and Aztec literature and in the elaborate forms of rhythm and repetition of Navaho chants. Canonical parallelism is thus a common feature of both oral poetry and ritual. But in ritual this device is combined with other types of formalisation in which speech, singing, gesture and dance are bound together in a compositional whole. Indeed, an event which did not contain all these elements would probably not be described by anthropologists as ritual; it is these features taken together that are ritual's distinguishing mark.

Compared with everyday speech, ritual speech is characterised not only by canonic parallelism but also by a restricted vocabulary, the exclusion of some syntactic forms, a fixity in the sequence of speech acts, fixed patterns in the volume of utterances, and a limited flexibility of intonation. All these features propel ritual speech acts in the same direction.[30] Thus any single utterance, instead of being followable by a large number of potential utterances, can be followed only by a limited set or indeed mostly by one utterance; the ending of a speech act is predictable from its beginning because, once begun, there is only one appropriate sequence along which one can properly proceed. Further, just as the linkages within a single speech act are formally predetermined, so too the linkages between the speech acts of different participants are determined in advance; from the speech act of one participant one can predict that of the next. Again, the choice of both intonation and of the rhythm of delivery are restricted in ritual speech. A further move, from intoned speech to song, consists in an ever more complete restriction of choice in intonation and rhythm, and in the adoption of an intonation and rhythm further removed still from the varied patterns of everyday speech. Finally, ritualised posture, gesture and movement, instead of flexibly combining to impart a variety and ambiguity of information as in what we conventionally describe as everyday situations, is restrictive in pattern, and hence easily predictable and easily repeatable, from one act to the next and from one ritual occasion to the next.

<h2 style="text-align:center">5</h2>

I turn now to the second difficulty: the tendency to ignore the pervasive importance in many cultures of actions which are explicitly represented as re-enactments of prior, prototypical actions. Commemorative ceremonies share two features of all other rituals, formalism and performativity; and in so far as they function effectively as mnemonic devices they are able to execute that function in large part because they possess such features. But commemorative ceremonies are distinguishable from all other rituals by the fact that they explicitly refer to prototypical persons and events, whether these are understood to have a historical or a mythological existence; and by virtue of that fact rites of this sort possess a further characteristic and one that is distinctively their own. We may describe this feature as that of ritual *re-enactment*, and it is a quality of cardinal importance in the shaping of communal memory. But the character of modern society and of modern self-understanding makes it singularly difficult for us to appreciate the nature of precisely this feature of ritual re-enactment. We may perhaps best seize hold of this characteristic of commemorative ceremonies if we approach it by juxtaposing two important statements, each of which seeks to delineate schematically a historically particular form of life and a way of understanding that type of life. The first figures centrally in Paul de Man's essay on 'Literary History and Literary Modernity'. The second is sketched out in Thomas Mann's address 'Freud and the Future'.

In 'Literary History and Literary Modernity' de Man fastens upon a particular type of forgetting as part of the core experience of modernity.[31] He invites us to consider 'the idea of modernity' as consisting in 'a desire to wipe out whatever came earlier, in the hope of reaching at last a point that would be called a true present, a point of origin that marks a new departure. This combined interplay of deliberate forgetting with an action that is also a new origin reaches the full power of the idea of modernity.'[32] The justification offered for this principled forgetting is automatically linked to what it negates: that is, to historicism. De Man more than acknowledges, he pointedly underscores, this paradox: the more radical the rejection of anything that came before, the greater the dependence on the past. We can develop de Man's insight by distinguishing two phases in the strategy of rejection. In the avant-garde it took the form of a rhetoric of forgetting, in postmodernism it appears as a rhetoric of pastiche. The attack of the avant-garde was directed mainly against the store-room of collective memory: museums, libraries and academies. The appeal to forget was at its most stridently uncompromising in the manifestos of the Futurists, who denounced intellectuals as the slaves of antiquated rites, museums as cemeteries, and libraries as burial chambers. But the Futurists were not alone; the idea of a tabula rasa had already been given a justification in Nietzsche and it recurred in the first third of this century in the work of avant-garde architects and town planners. In postmodernism this stance is superseded by the omnipresence of pastiche in which the past is seen as a vast collection of images, all styles of the past being potentially open to the play of random, often humorous, allusion. In a world characterised by what Henri Lefebvre has called the increasing primacy of the 'neo', the past as a referent is gradually effaced.[33]

In 'Freud and the Future' Thomas Mann coaxed his audience into imaginatively envisaging a form of life and a way of thinking about that life which is modernity's polar opposite.[34] We are to envisage the ego, less sharply defined and less exclusive than we commonly conceive of it, as being so to speak 'open behind': open to the resources of myth which are to be understood as existing for the individual not just as a grid of categories but as a set of possibilities which can become subjective, which can be lived consciously. In this archaising attitude the life of the individual is consciously lived as a 'sacred repetition', as the explicit reanimation of prototypes. Thus Alexander consciously walked in the footsteps of Miltiades; thus the ancient biographers of Caesar were convinced that he took Alexander as his prototype; and thus the life of Christ is represented in the Gospels as a life lived in order that what was written might be fulfilled. Thus too, in conscious modern archaism, the fundamental motif of *Joseph and His Brothers* is the idea of an individual life as an act of identification, as a conscious moving in another's footsteps. For Joseph's teacher, Eliezer, time is cancelled as all the Eliezers of the past gather together to shape the Eliezer of the present, so that he comes to speak in the first person of that Eliezer who was Abraham's servant, although he was far from being the same man. And in the chapter 'The Great Hoaxing', what the author calls a 'mythical recurrent farce' is tragicomically played out by a group of persons, Isaac, Esau and Jacob, all of whom already know well in whose steps they tread. Mann speaks of the style and structure of an individual life evoked here as 'a kind of celebration', as 'the performance by a celebrant of a prescribed procedure'.

This is a way of envisaging the pattern of an individual's life that is not readily comprehensible to us. When we think of elements of an individual's life as being recurrent, we are likely to be prompted to do so by one of two characteristically modern lines of thought. We may bracket individual variety out of the equation because we see the significantly recurrent as that which is statistically typical. Or we may train our attention on what is repeated unconsciously because we see the significantly recurrent as that which undermines the project of individual autonomy. In either case what we will characteristically lose from sight is any sense that the recurrent and typical in the structure of an individual life is significant because it traces out a pattern that is to be celebrated; that individuals might celebrate their role and realise their value exclusively in the knowledge that it is a fresh incarnation of the traditional; that by consciously repeating the past an individual life gives the past presentness again. The sense of this was peculiarly familiar to antiquity, but it is accessible to us, for the most part, only at secondhand, by reference to the example of antiquity. We might refer to this pre-modern self-understanding as a kind of imitation so long as we remember that imitation here means far more than we mean by the word today. It means something like mythical identification.

The idea of a form of life which draws its significance from the performance by celebrants of prescribed procedures, from the reanimation of prototypes, may at all times be physically possible and may still be operative under contemporary conditions. Modern invented rites mark the traces of this possibility, the attempts to revive the sense of life as ritual re-enactment in secular vocabulary. Particularly between 1870 and 1914 European countries saw an efflorescence of invented rites. Royal jubilees, Bastille Day and the Internationale, the Olympic Games, the Cup Final and the Tour de France: all seek to restore in a new form the celebration of the exemplary recurrent. Nor were such celebrations confined to the period of their most sustained invention. Even now, most of the occasions when citizens are made conscious of their membership of states, as in elections, remain associated with historically new semi-ritual practices; while new types of formal ritual spaces for the purposes of semi-official spectacle, such as sports stadia, retain their aura. On semi-official as on official occasions the elaboration of a theatrical idiom of public symbolic discourse continues in effect. Such occasions, it is true, no longer make imaginatively available to us that strong sense of imitation as mythical identification which Mann so powerfully evokes; but they do still produce and provide shape for a communal desire – a wish to repeat the past consciously, to find significance in celebrated recurrence.

The celebration of recurrence is no monopoly of traditional societies. But the celebration of recurrence is a compensatory device. Capitalism, in Marx's famous phrase, tears down all social immobility, every ancestral confinement and feudal restriction; and invented rites, however implicated they often are in that very process of modernisation which capitalism drives remorselessly on, are palliative measures, façades erected to screen off the full implications of this vast worldwide clearing operation. Newly invented rites spring up and are instantly formalised in acknowledgement of the global historical break. That is why invented rites, involving sets of recorded rules and procedures, as in modern coronation rites, are marked out by their inflexibility. By virtue of their procedural inflexibility they are held to represent, as nowhere else, the idea of the unchanging for a society of institutionalised innovation. Their intention is reassurance and their mood is nostalgic. It is not, therefore, the experience of recapitulative imitation, of mythic identification, but the display of formal structure that is the most evident mark of such rites.

Under the conditions of modernity the celebration of recurrence can never be anything more than a compensatory strategy, because the very principle of modernity itself denies the idea of life as a structure of celebrated recurrence. It denies credence to the thought that the life of an individual or a community either can or should derive its value from acts of consciously performed recall, from the reliving of the prototypical. Although the process of modernisation does indeed generate invented rituals as compensatory devices, the logic of modernisation erodes those conditions which make acts of ritual re-enactment, of recapitulative imitation, imaginatively possible and persuasive. For the essence of modernity is economic development, the vast transformation of society precipitated by the emergence of the capitalist world market. And capital accumulation, the ceaseless expansion of the commodity form through the market, requires the constant revolutionising of production, the ceaseless transformation of the innovative into the obsolescent. The clothes people wear, the machines they operate, the workers who service the machines, the neighbourhoods they live in – all are constructed today to be dismantled tomorrow, so that they can be replaced or recycled. Integral to the accumulation of capital is the repeated intentional destruction of the built environment.[35] Integral too is the transformation of all signs of cohesion into rapidly changing fashions of costume, language and practice. The temporality of the market and of the commodities that circulate through it generates an experience of time as quantitative and as flowing in a single direction, an experience in which each moment is different from the other by virtue of coming next, situated in a chronological succession of old and new, earlier and later. The temporality of the market thus denies the possibility that there might co-exist qualitatively distinguishable times, a profane time and a sacred time, neither of which is reducible to the other.[36] The operation of this system brings about a massive withdrawal of credence in the possibility that there might exist forms of life that are exemplary because prototypical. The logic of capital tends to deny the capacity any longer to imagine life as a structure of exemplary recurrence.

When, on the other hand, everyday life is envisaged as a structure of exemplary recurrences, the imaginative persuasiveness of such a perception is wrought through what may be called *a rhetoric of re-enactment*. This rhetoric works by employing at least three distinguishable modes of articulation: we might call them calendrical, verbal and gestural re-enactment.

The celebration of recurrence is made possible, in the first instance, by *calendrically* observed repetition. Calendars make it possible to juxtapose with the structure of profane time a further structure, one qualitatively distinct from the former and irreducible to it, in which the most notable events of sacred time are assembled together and co-ordinated.[37] Each day is thus locatable in two quite different orders of time: there is the day on which such and such events take place in the world, and there is the day on which one celebrates the memory of this or that moment of a sacred or mythic history. While the co-existence of these two temporal orders runs through the course of the entire calendrical cycle, that cycle will normally contain special points at which the activity of recapitulation becomes the special focus of communal attention. New Year is celebrated in most religions by ceremonies in which reference is made to a cosmogonic myth. Throughout the semitic world, in particular, the ceremonials of the New Year are strikingly similar.[38] In each of these systems, we encounter the same basic idea of an annual return to chaos followed by a new creation. In each, there is expressed the conception of the end and the beginning of a temporal period, based on the observation of biocosmic rhythms, and celebrated in a sequence of periodic purifications – purgings, fastings, confessions of sins – in preparation for the periodic regeneration of life. And in each, the ritual enactment of combats between two groups of actors, the presence of the dead, and saturnalia, gives expression to the sense that the end of the old year and the expectation of the new year is at once an annual repetition and the repetition of a primordial moment – the mythic moment of the passage from chaos to cosmos. Every New Year is interpreted as a calendrical repetition of the cosmogonic act. The New Year scenario of a repeated creation is particularly explicit in all cultures of the Middle East, in Babylon and Egypt, Israel and Iran. But Christianity too never envisaged the material sequence of the natural cycle otherwise than as the pattern and symbol of a hidden order: only that the emphasis shifts in this schema from the prototype of creation to that of salvation. Thus one of the central preoccupations of early Christianity was the determination of the date of Easter, the feast which annually perpetuates, on the one hand, the Jewish Passover and the Paschal sacrifice, and, on the other, the sacrifice of Calvary and the Resurrection of Christ.[39] It was considered imperative that this feast be celebrated at exactly the same point of time in the annual cycle as the events which it repeated. In this as in other religions the certainty that particular events were inserted into a recapitulative structure enjoyed a kind of echo-effect from the perceived order of a cosmic sequence.

Calendars make possible the distinction between a time built up of units that are quantitatively equivalent and a time composed of units that are qualitatively identical. To understand commemorative celebration we need to hold in mind this distinction between equivalence and identity. The notion of time in commemorative rites is not that of a pure quantity; the parts of time are not conceived as being indefinitely divisible into successive units in an irreversible linear sequence. Rather, the intervals which are framed by certain critical dates, and which annually occupy the same relative position in the calendar, are believed to be qualitatively similar; the homogeneity of such phases is demonstrated by the fact that chronological similarity entails or permits the repetition of the same actions. The same enactments and the same representations are attached to these ritual periods in such a way that they can be made to appear to be the exact reproduction of each other. The same religious or magical rites are accomplished in the same temporal circumstances, that is at the symmetrically identical points of a system, whatever that system may be, which divides up time. The same feasts are celebrated on the same dates. With each periodical festival the participants thus find themselves as it were in the same time: the same that had been manifested in the festival of the previous year, or in that of a century, or five centuries earlier. These critical intervals are organised so as to appear and be experienced as qualitatively identical. By its very nature, therefore, ritual time is indefinitely repeatable.

The rhetoric of re-enactment is encoded too in *verbal* repetition. In the ceremonies of Judaism, Christianity and Islam, of Buddhism and Hinduism, sacred words are uttered in the language of an authorised sacred text. Most of the world religions, in consequence, are marked by a disjunction between a profane and a religious language.[40] Latin in the Catholic Church, Hebrew for Jews, Vedic Sanskrit for Hindus and Arabic for Muslims, all are sacred languages whose difference from the language of ordinary language must be pronounced. Within this common area of assumption, there is room for some variation regarding the nature of the authority ascribed to the sacred language and the degrees of its linguistic exclusiveness. An extreme position is represented by Muslims for whom the Koran is efficacious only in the original Arabic, and by Jews for whom the Word of God is in Hebrew. A more flexible position is found in

Christianity, which never claimed that any part of the Bible was originally written in Latin; yet here too, in practice, Latin had supplanted Greek as the language of worship by the end of the third century; from then on it was considered to be the holy language of the Western church and, until 1967, the Catholic Church held to the view that religious rites should be uttered in the language of the Latin liturgy. Nor is the break between a language of sacred recitation and a more formless profane language confined to the world religions; many preliterate peoples, for instance the Trobriands and the Kachin, who recite their religious mythology in sagas, do so in archaic form of speech hardly comprehensible to contemporary speakers. In preliterate as in literate societies sacred languages contain an archaic component, whether in the form of a totally different language or whether in the partial preservation of another idiom; and this archaic component remains so long as rites refer back to a period of revelation and insist on the authority of true texts properly transmitted either orally or in written form. The question as to whether the participants in the rite understand the words is then secondary and is not considered to affect the efficacy of the ritual. What matters is that rites must manifest the gift of tongues. The recitation of gospels and psalms, of prayers and sagas, has the same ritual value – as repeatable utterances – as have a genuflection or an offering, a gesture of benediction or a ceremonial dance. It is of the essence of sacred utterances that they should have been submitted to a minimum of modifications since their origin. Their efficacy is in their uttered repetition.

When it takes place as part of what I have called the rhetoric of re-enactment, verbal repetition possesses a distinctive feature. One way of trying to grasp what this consists of is to compare it with other instances of apparently total repetition. There is a certain type of repetition which we are familiar with when a film or recorded music or a work of literature is perceived by us for the second time or several times. The repetition of such works, which do not require within the work itself the mediation of interpreters, is in an important way analogous to the repetition of words, for instance in theatrical performances, where the mediation of such interpreters is required; for just as the repeated performance of the same play by different actors at different times accentuates the specific nature of each performance and brings to our attention the differences between these performances, so also, even if in a qualitatively different way, the 'repeated' perception of the same text or recorded disc or film discloses the development of the perceiver's consciousness and brings to our attention the differences in each reading. In these cases the total repetition is only apparent. But we encounter a different phenomenon when, for example, we find that in some of its parts Christian liturgy repeats texts which announce, as an event that is to come or as an event that has already occurred in the life of Jesus Christ, a narrative of salvation. The relationship here between the individual occasions of verbal repetition is unlike that which applies to an art-work whose individual performances can be repeated; nor is the relationship between the individual occurrences of the rite and its founding act paralleled in the relationship between the individual performances of the art-work and their first performance. Verbal re-enactment here is a special kind of actualisation, and it is in its sacramental aspect that liturgical language has its most evidently actualising quality. In repeating the words of the Last Supper, for instance, the celebrant is held to repeat once again that which Jesus Christ did, in giving again to the words which Christ used the same efficacy which Christ gave them, by conferring on those words again the power to do what they mean. There is, first of all, the primary performativity, by means of which Christ enabled certain words to do what they meant. And there is, in addition, what we may call a secondary or sacramental performativity, by virtue of which the celebrant, in repeating those words in the context of the prayer of the canon, is held to be restoring to them their primary performativity. In verbal re-enactment of this kind we have embodied, not indeed total repetition, but the idea of total repetition.

The rhetoric of re-enactment is encoded too in an even more direct embodiment, in *gestural* repetition. Particularly in archaic rituals this process comes most starkly into play in the represented presence of the dead. Among the Luapala, the elders use the first person singular when speaking for their dead predecessors; and this identification through utterance reaches its full bodily culmination with possession, during the course of which the particular individual elder ceases to exist, as it were, and is replaced by 'another'.[41] Among the Yuma Indians of Colorado, actors imitate the heroic deeds and gestures of ancestors, wearing masks that represent, and in this way identify them with, these ancestors; the active presence of beings from the primordial creative period is conjured up, for they alone are credited with the magic quality that can confer the desired efficacy upon the rite. Caillois underlines the cognitive reach of such gestural repetition when he remarks that in these instances no unequivocal distinction can be made between 'the mythical base of the ceremony and the actual ceremony';[42] and Daryll Forde has shown the consequence of such a phenomenon in the case of the Yuma, among whom his informants continually confused the rite that they were accustomed to celebrate with the act through which their ancestors were held to have originally instituted it.[43] Again, in the kingdom of Uganda, a way was found of keeping the spirit of the dead king among his subjects in representative form. After his death a medium, or *mandura*, was nominated in whom the spirit of the dead king took up its dwelling; this medium reproduced not only the exact appearance but the speech and gestures of the dead king. In clans responsible for providing *manduras* the characteristics of each king at the time of his death were handed down orally and mimetically, so that whenever a *mandura* died another of the same clan took over the office and the spirit of the king was never without a representative. This representative did not enact the dead king continuously, but from time to time the medium became possessed and embodied the king in every detail.[44] More generally, in nearly all ceremonial dances the wearers of masks represent 'ghosts', that is, in most cases, the spirits of the dead. Lévy-Bruhl has stressed that the word 'represent' must be understood here in its literal etymological sense: meaning to re-present, to cause to reappear that which has disappeared.[45] To wear a mask is to have immediate and direct contact with the beings of the unseen world; during the time of such direct contact the individuality of the actor and of the spirit he represents are one. For as long as the actors and dancers wear these masks, and from the fact that they cover their faces, they are not only the representatives of the dead, they 'become' ancestors whom these masks portray – for the time being, they actually 'become' the dead and their ancestors. In such archaic rituals gestural repetition enacts the idea of bi-presence; the inhabitants of the other world can reappear in this one without leaving their own, provided one knows how to recall them.

The idea of representation as a re-presenting, as causing to reappear that which has disappeared, is not confined to the rites of preliterate peoples. It is expressed too in commemorations as otherwise divergent in structure and tone as the Muharram festival of the Shiites and the liturgy of Catholicism: both re-enact a holy narrative by gestural repetitions, in the one case through an orchestration of frenzied grief, in the other through a slow choreography of calm and ordered sequence. The Muharram festival of the Shiites re-enacts the occasion when Husain and his men, who were of 'the family of the Prophet', were attacked and killed on the plain of Kerbela in the year 680.[46] Shiites keep the anniversary of Kerbela on the tenth day – Ashura – of the month of Muharram; they mourn the fate of Husain in figurative re-enactment. During the first nine days of this month, officials are dressed in black or grey; soldiers and mule-drivers go about with their shirts hanging down and their chests bare, which is understood as a sign of great grief; groups of them wander the streets, wounding themselves with swords, dragging chains behind them, and performing frenzied dances. On the tenth of Muharram the festival culminates in a gigantic procession designed as a funerary parade to re-enact the burial of Husain; his coffin is carried by eight men and flanked on either side by men bearing banners; behind the coffin follow sixty blood-stained men singing a warlike song;

behind them again are a group of others who beat wooden staves rhyth-
mically against each other. The pain they inflict on themselves figuratively
exhibits the pain of Husain. It is difficult to imagine a set of rites further
removed from this than that of Catholic liturgy, characterised as it is by a
tone of calm solemnity. Yet here too everything turns upon the fact that the
liturgy is not propositional statement but sacred action. These actions
convey conviction by incorporating it. Not the pulpit but the altar is the
privileged site. In the pulpit the sacred narrative receives a commentary; at
the altar the substance of the narrative is communicated in physical signs
that contain it. Rites are woven out of scriptural allusion and many liturgical gestures reproduce those mentioned in the Bible.[47] The eating of bread
in Communion, the immersion in water at baptism, the laying on of hands
in confirmation and ordination, the sign of the Cross – all are figurative
repetitions. These ritual movements preserve: while physical existence is
quintessentially transient, ritual gestures remain identical. Wherever they
are repeated the reference is to a biblical narrative and, more specifically
still, to the Jerusalem of Easter: the liturgy is, as it were, the permanent
making present of that temporal situation. What we witness here is not the
abandonment of the idea of bi-presence; rather, gestural mimesis is translated, as it were, from a realistic to a symbolic mode; one genre of mimetic
re-enactment replaces another.

I have considered those features which commemorative ceremonies
share with other rituals of an extended and elaborated kind. In doing so I
approached ritual not as a type of symbolic representation but as a species
of performative; and to this end contrasted myths, as reservoirs of possibility on which variations can be played, and rituals, on which no such
variation is permissible. I then went on to consider those features which
mark off commemorative ceremonies as performances of a distinctive
kind. In doing so I underlined the cultural pervasiveness of performances
which explicitly re-enact other actions that are represented as prototypical;
and to this end I itemised the rhetoric of that re-enactment, calendrical,
verbal and gestural.

What, then, is being remembered in commemorative ceremonies? Part
of the answer is that a community is reminded of its identity as represented
by and told in a master narrative. This is a collective variant of what I earlier
called personal memory, that is to say a making sense of the past as a kind
of collective autobiography, with some explicitly cognitive components.
But rituals are not just further instances of humanity's now much touted
propensity to explain the world to itself by telling stories. A ritual is not a
journal or memoir. Its master narrative is more than a story told and
reflected on; it is a cult enacted. An image of the past, even in the form of a
master narrative, is conveyed and sustained by ritual performances. And

this means that what is remembered in commemorative ceremonies is something in addition to a collectively organised variant of personal and cognitive memory. For if the ceremonies are to work for their participants, if they are to be persuasive to them, then those participants must be not simply cognitively competent to execute the performance; they must be habituated to those performances. This habituation is to be found – in ways about which I shall have more to say subsequently – in the bodily substrate of the performance.

I have sought to analyse commemorative ceremonies until they yield the bodiliness that is their substrate. My argument is that, if there is such a thing as social memory, we are likely to find it in commemorative ceremonies. Commemorative ceremonies prove to be commemorative (only) in so far as they are performative. But performative memory is in fact much more widespread than commemorative ceremonies which are – though performance is necessary to them – highly representational. Performative memory is bodily. Therefore, I want to argue, there is an aspect of social memory which has been greatly neglected but is absolutely essential: bodily social memory.

3

Bodily practices

1

We preserve versions of the past by representing it to ourselves in words and images. Commemorative ceremonies are pre-eminent instances of this. They keep the past in mind by a depictive representation of past events. They are re-enactments of the past, its return in a representational guise which normally includes a simulacrum of the scene or situation recaptured. Such re-enactments depend for much of their rhetorical persuasiveness, as we have seen, on prescribed bodily behaviour. But we can also preserve the past deliberately without explicitly re-presenting it in words and images. Our bodies, which in commemorations stylistically re-enact an image of the past, keep the past also in an entirely effective form in their continuing ability to perform certain skilled actions. We may not remember how or when we first learned to swim, but we can keep on swimming successfully – remembering how to do it – without any representational activity on our part at all; we consult a mental picture of what we should do when our capacity to execute spontaneously the bodily movements in question is defective. Many forms of habitual skilled remembering illustrate a keeping of the past in mind that, without ever adverting to its historical origin, nevertheless re-enacts the past in our present conduct. In habitual memory the past is, as it were, sedimented in the body.

In suggesting more particularly how memory is sedimented, or amassed, in the body, I want to distinguish between two fundamentally different types of social practice.

The first type of action I shall call an *incorporating* practice. Thus a smile or a handshake or words spoken in the presence of someone we address, are all messages that a sender or senders impart by means of their own current bodily activity, the transmission occurring only during the time that their bodies are present to sustain that particular activity. Whether the information imparted by these actions is conveyed intentionally or unintentionally, and whether it is carried by an individual or a group, I shall speak of such actions as incorporated.

The second type of action I shall call an *inscribing* practice. Thus our modern devices for storing and retrieving information, print, encyclopedias, indexes, photographs, sound tapes, computers, all require that we do something that traps and holds information, long after the human organism has stopped informing. Occasionally this imparting may be unintentional, as when we have our telephone tapped, but mostly it is intentional. I shall speak of all such actions as inscribing.

The memorisation of culturally specific postures may be taken as an example of incorporating practices. In a culture where the characteristic postures of men and women are nearly identical, there may be very little teaching of posture and very little conscious learning of posture.[1] But whenever postural differences are introduced, for example, between the postures appropriate for ceremonial occasions and for everyday activities or between the modes of sitting appropriate for males and females, some awareness of postural appropriateness is involved. For instance, in one culture the correct seated posture for a woman may be with her legs drawn under her and to one side, and the correct seated posture for a man may be cross-legged. Little boys and girls will be corrected, verbally or by gesture, but most corrections will probably take the form of uttering phrases such as 'girls don't sit like that' or 'sit like a man'. The ability to disapprove must be among the first teaching abilities in the effort to establish a transmissible culture; and further refinements will come with the ability to name a culturally correct posture, with words for squat, kneel, bow, stand erect, and so on, combined with pointing to specific forms of correct and incorrect behaviour. Postural behaviour, then, may be very highly structured and completely predictable, even though it is neither verbalised nor consciously taught and may be so automatic that it is not even recognised as isolatable pieces of behaviour. The presence of living models, the presence, that is, of men and women actually sitting 'correctly', is essential to the communication in question.

The importance of postures for communal memory is evident. Power and rank are commonly expressed through certain postures relative to others; from the way in which people group themselves and from the disposition of their bodies relative to the bodies of others, we can deduce the degree of authority which each is thought to enjoy or to which they lay claim. We know what it means when one person sits in an elevated position when everyone around them stands; when one person stands and everyone else sits; when everyone in a room gets up as someone comes in; when someone bows, or curtseys, or, in extreme circumstances, falls to their knees before another who remains standing. These are only some of the many configurations of communal activity. There will of course be disparities between cultures in the meanings ascribed to some postures, but, in all cultures, much of the choreography of authority is expressed through the body. Within this choreography, there is an identifiable range of repertoires through which many postural performances become meaningful by registering meaningful inflections of the upright posture.[2] Such inflections recall a pattern of authority to performers and observers, and they are in turn recalled to mind in many of our verbal conventions. This is evident in our common metaphors. When we speak of someone as being 'upright' we may use the expression descriptively and literally to mean that they are standing on their own feet, or we may use it evaluatively and metaphorically to express admiration and praise of someone whom we judge to be honest and just, to be loyal to friends in difficulties, to stand by their own convictions, and in general not to stoop to low or unworthy actions. When we refer to someone who enjoys a high social position, we say that they have 'status' or 'standing'. When we speak of misfortunes of all kinds we express the change of circumstances as a fall; we fall into the enemy's hands, we fall upon hard times, we fall from favour. Nor are such metaphoric turns of phrase ad hoc; they remind us of patterns of authority because they form not simply individual metaphoric turns of phrase but whole systems of metaphoric expression.[3] Our oppositional concepts 'up' and 'down' arise out of our bodily experience of verticality. Almost every bodily movement we make changes our up-down orientation, maintains it, or in some way takes it into account. The direction upwards, against gravity, establishes the postural base in our experience of lived space for the dichotomous sense to which we attach values, such as those expressed in the oppositions between high and low, rise and decline, climbing and falling, superior and inferior, looking up to and looking down upon. It is through the essentially embodied nature of our social existence, and through the incorporated practices based upon these embodyings, that these oppositional terms provide us with metaphors by which we think and live. Culturally specific postural performances provide us with a mnemonics of the body.

The alphabet may be cited, by contrast, as an example of an inscribing practice. It is a practice that exists by virtue of a systematic transfer from the temporal properties of the human voice to the spatial properties of the inscribed marks: that is, to replicable features of their form, position, actual distances, order and linear disposition.[4] Other writing systems – pictograms, hieroglyphics and ideograms – exhibit the same characteristic; but their methods of spatial encoding are radically incomplete because they are still dependent on a direct inscription of meanings. That is why pictograms, for instance, are so deficient as mnemonic systems: a vast number of signs are needed to represent all the objects in the culture; the simplest sentence requires an elaborate series of signs; and only a limited number of things can be said. Limited writing systems of this kind, in which the sign directly represents the referent, are of course capable of semantic extension; the same sign can be made to stand also for a more general class of objects or for other referents connected with the original sign by association of meaning. Thus in Egyptian hieroglyphics the sign for a beetle was a code sign not only for that insect but also for a separate and more abstract referent 'because'. But since all such methods of inscriptional elaboration remain arbitrary, the interpretation of their signs is neither easy nor explicit. In Chinese writing a minimum of 3,000 characters has to be learned before one is reasonably literate, and there exists in all a repertoire of 50,000 characters to be mastered. The phonetic principle marks a decisive break with all such procedures. What distinguishes it from all other writing systems is the fact that the twenty-two components out of which the system is constructed have in themselves no intrinsic meaning. The names of the Greek letters, alpha, beta, gamma and so on, make up a nursery chant designed to imprint the sounds of the letters in a fixed series on the child's brain while firmly correlating the sounds with the child's vision of a fixed series of shapes which they look at when they produce the acoustic values. In their original Semitic form these names were names of common objects like 'house', 'camel', and so on; in Greek the names have become meaningless. When the component units of the system were in this way voided of any independent meaning, they were transformed into a mechanical mnemonic device. This device imposed a habit of recognition on the brain in the developmental phase before puberty while the oral language code was being acquired. The two codes needed for speaking and then for reading combine together at a time when mental resources are still extremely malleable, so that the acts of reading and writing become an unconscious reflex. The cultural break established by the phonetic principle thus has decisive ontogenetic significance.

The impact of writing on social memory is much written about and evidently vast.[5] The transition from an oral culture to a literate culture is a transition from incorporating practices to inscribing practices. The impact of writing depends upon the fact that any account which is transmitted by means of inscriptions is unalterably fixed, the process of its composition being definitively closed. The standard edition and the canonic work are the emblems of this condition. This fixity is the spring that releases innovation. When the memories of a culture begin to be transmitted mainly by the reproduction of their inscriptions rather than by 'live' tellings, improvisation becomes increasingly difficult and innovation is institutionalised.

Phonetic writing generates cultural innovation by promoting two processes: economisation and scepticism. Economisation: because the form of communal memory is freed from its dependence on rhythm.[6] Scepticism: because the content of communal memory is subjected to systematic criticism.[7] With regard to economisation, we may note that in oral cultures most of the formal recollection of happenings takes the form of performances repeatedly recited by the custodians of memory to those who hear of it. These large-scale performative utterances have to be cast in a standardised form if there is to be any chance of their being repeated by successive generations; and the rhythms of oral verse are the privileged mechanisms of recall because rhythm enlists the co-operation of a whole series of bodily motor reflexes in the work of remembrance. But rhythm sets drastic limits to the verbal arrangement of what might be said and thought. Phonetic writing breaks down these limitations. By substituting a visual record for an acoustic one, the alphabet frees a society from the constraints of a rhythmic mnemonics. Particular statements need no longer be memorised but can lie around as artefacts and be consulted as required. This economisation of memory releases extensive mental energies previously invested in the construction and preservation of mnemonic systems; hence it encourages the production of unfamiliar statements and the thinking of novel thoughts. With regard to scepticism, we may note that in oral cultures much of the informal recollection of happenings takes the form of face-to-face conversation. This necessarily impedes the articulation of a sense of inconsistency or even incoherence in the fabric of the cultural inheritance. It is true that oral societies often make a distinction between the folktale, the myth, and the historical legend. But even if inconsistency occurs between or within such genres, it is unlikely that the sense of inconsistency will generate a permanent cultural impact. Scepticism is particular, not culturally accumulative; it generates titular disputes, but not a deliberate reinterpretation of the cultural inheritance. The distinction between what was held to be mythical and what was considered to be historical came into being when it became possible to set one fixed account of the world beside another so that the contradictions within and between them could literally be seen. Through criticism as well as through economisation, the substance of communal memory is changed by the transformation in the technology of preserved communication.

A hesitancy is bound to arise as soon as these distinctions have been made. For it is certainly the case that many practices of inscription contain an element of incorporation, and it may indeed be that no type of inscription is at all conceivable without such an irreducible incorporating aspect.

It is certainly true that writing, the most obvious example of inscription, has an irreducible bodily component. We tend to forget this; writing is a habitual exercise of intelligence and volition which normally escapes the notice of the person exercising it because of this familiarity with the method of procedure. Everyone who can write proficiently knows how to form each letter so well and knows so well each word they are about to write that they have ceased to be conscious of this knowledge or to notice these particular acts of volition. Each of these acts, none the less, is accompanied by a corresponding muscular action.[8] The way in which we generally adhere to the same method of forming the same character in handwriting demonstrates that writing entails a minimal muscular skill; and if we begin to write in an unfamiliar way, as when printing our letters instead of writing them longhand, we will be alerted to the fact that every character we form entails a bodily action. None the less, there is a good reason for picking out the inscriptional element in writing as its predominant feature. For when we learn to write, the physical movements we make have no meaning of their own but are contingently required to form the shapes that are themselves merely arbitrarily related to meaning. This contingency of the hand movements involved is well displayed by the use of the typewriter, where the registration of the same signs requires different bodily movements.

We could of course consider a quite different case where the practice of good handwriting is conceived of as part of the training of a docile body. Here disciplinary control consists in imposing the best relation between a set of gestures and the overall position of the body, which is its condition of efficiency and speed. This is not a hypothetical but a historical example: in his inventory of surveillances Foucault cites the disciplinarian La Salle, who talks about a training in handwriting in which a disciplined body is the prerequisite of an efficient set of gestures. Pupils, he says, must always 'hold their bodies erect, somewhat turned and free on the left side, slightly inclined, so that, with the elbow placed on the table, the chin can be rested upon the hand unless this were to interfere with the view; the left leg must be somewhat more forward under the table than the right. A distance of two fingers must be left between the body and the table; for not only does one write with more alertness, but nothing is more harmful to the health than to acquire the habit of pressing one's stomach against the table; the part of the left arm from the elbow to the hand must be placed on the table. The right arm must be at a distance from the body of about three fingers and be about five fingers from the table, on which it must rest lightly. The teacher will place the pupils in the posture that they should maintain when writing, and will correct it either by sign or otherwise, when they change this position.'[9] La Salle is here proposing a training in rigorous docility, a kind of minuscule gymnastics. The essential point is that what is being prescribed and learnt is an incorporating practice. It also happens to be a practice of inscription; but that is a contingent feature of the practice in question, for, fundamentally, what is being learned is an act of incorporation.

The same point applies less obviously but no less certainly to the institution of the cinema. To say that cinema is an inscribing practice is to single out that feature which marks it off from theatre.[10] In theatre, actors and spectators are present at the same time and in the same location; everything the audience see and hear is actively produced in their presence by human beings or props which are themselves present. In cinema, the actors were present when the spectators were absent (at the shooting) and the actors are absent when the spectators are present (at the projection). Not only am I at a distance from the object, as in theatre; what remains in that distance, in cinema, is no longer the object itself, which is inaccessible from the outset, but, as Metz puts it, a delegate it has sent me while itself withdrawing. What defines the rules of looking specific to cinema is the absence of the object seen. The absence of the object and the codes by which we make sense of that absence are produced by the process of technical inscription. The cinema inscribes; but it could not be a practice of inscription if it were not also, in a specific sense, an incorporating practice. What is incorporated is an ocular convention: the identification of the object with the camera. During the cinema performance spectators duplicate the action of the projector, their eyes behaving as it were like searchlights. Without this identification with the camera certain facts would remain unintelligible: for example, the fact that the spectators are not puzzled when the images on the screen 'rotate' in a panning movement, yet the spectators know that they have not turned their heads. The spectators do not need to turn their heads really; for they have turned their heads in so far as they have identified themselves as all-seeing subjects with the movement of the camera. If the eye which thus moves is no longer bound by the laws of matter, if the eye is in this sense no longer bound to the body but has become capable of multiple displacements, then the world, in cinema, will not only be constituted by the eye, in the sense in which the eye-subject formed the invisible basis of Quattrocento perspective, but the world will be constituted for the eye. This marks a turning point in the social formation of the eye. In cinema, I am simultaneously in this action and outside of it, in this space and outside of this space; having the power of ubiquity, I am everywhere and nowhere. The inscriptional practice of cinema makes possible, and is in turn made possible by, the incorporating practice of the cinema spectator.

Many practices of inscription contain an element of incorporation, and it may even be the case that no type of inscription at all is conceivable without such an irreducible component of incorporation. I take the distinction between incorporating and inscribing practices to serve the end of my argument, none the less, in so far as it is possible to distinguish between actions in which the one or the other aspect predominates. My classification is intended, in other words, as a heuristic device.

2

The incorporating practices I have in mind are generally characterised by a lesser degree of formality than that which is found in those highly invariant events, like certain religious liturgies, in which almost all of the performance is specified in advance and where the occasions for variation are few and closely defined. But within this range of activities there are different types of culturally specific bodily practices which will differ from one another in the degree of formality characteristic of them. There is of course some difficulty in distinguishing bodily practices in terms of the criterion of formality. Recurrent events cannot always be easily separated into those which are formal and those which are not. They occupy, rather, shifting areas along a continuum. There is a continuance of behavioural formality from the formal words and gestures that intersperse ordinary conversation and everyday events; through everyday formalities of greeting behaviour and formal expressions of deference and demeanour; through the fairly invariant procedures of, say, the courtroom within which the variable substance of litigation is contained by the means which subject it to ordered presentation; to, finally, such events as coronations, in which the invariant aspects of the event begin to predominate over its variable aspects. It is impossible, then, to distinguish unequivocally between qualitatively distinct kinds of formality. What I wish to suggest here are a set of merely heuristic distinctions: a distinction between ceremonies of the body, proprieties of the body, and techniques of the body.

As an example of *techniques* of the body we might consider the case of gesture. A particularly illuminating instance is provided by David Efron, who set out to examine whether there were any standardised and classifiable differences in gestural behaviour between groups.[11] He proposed this question with respect to two subgroups, 'traditional' East European Jews and Southern Italians living in New York; by 'traditional' he meant both foreign and American-born individuals who had retained the language and customs of their original group and who had remained entirely impervious to the influence of the American environment. As a method of investigation, he rejected laboratory controls in favour of natural settings; all his material was obtained in spontaneous situations in the everyday environment of the people concerned, who did not know that they were the subjects of his study. As an object of investigation, he ruled

out any consideration of facial expression, posture, gait, or eye movements; his focus was mainly on hand movements and to a lesser extent on
head movements. This limited focus of attention was justified by the
common-sense observation that both immigrant groups 'talked with their
hands' in ways evidently not the case with the surrounding society; but it
turned out upon scrutiny that this was so in strikingly different and
definable senses with respect to the two groups in question.

From the data collected in the Italian quarter of New York Efron was able
to build up a more or less exhaustive inventory of the 'bundle of pictures'
that traditional Southern Italians carry in their hands. This amounted in
effect to a lexicon, a gestural vocabulary comprising at least a hundred and
fifty items. Some of these formalised movements can also be found in the
repertoire of other groups; others are local, their meaning being clear only
to a member of a traditional Southern Italian community or to someone
who is familiar with its system of bodily signs. These movements are, as it
were, manual 'words' designating more or less definite meaningful
associations; they illustrate the very things referred to by the accompanying words. Southern Italian gestural behaviour is substantive in character,
in the sense that it contains a large number of visuo-spatial replicas of the
referents of thought. The production of such gestural 'slides' can, when
pushed to the limit, concatenate into an entire 'slide-show' in which verbal
accompaniment is dispensed with. Cardinal Manning had long before
been amazed at the capacity of Sicilians to carry on a complete conversation without the aid of a single spoken word; and Efron too was struck by
the appearance of long sequences of pantomimic gestures when several
prominent Italian actors in New York evidently had not the least difficulty
in enacting a series of 'dumb-shows' which were entirely meaningful to
anyone acquainted with the system of gestural pictures and symbols
employed by their group. More impressive even than the self-sufficiency
of this lexical repertoire was its longevity. Over a century earlier, Andrea di
Jorio had produced an exhaustive description of the gestural vocabulary of
the traditional Neapolitan in his *La Mimica degli Antichi Investigata nel
Gestire Napoletano*.[12] Many of the gestures described by di Jorio are still in
use among contemporary Neapolitans in Italy as well as in the United
States. And some can be traced as far back as ancient Greece and Rome, as
can be seen by comparing Efron's gestural charts with the descriptions and
pictorial reproductions of Greek and Roman gestures provided both by di
Jorio and by Karl Sittl.[13] Several of the hand movements included in Efron's
collection are recognisable in Quintilian's description of Roman oratorical
gestures.

Whereas the traditional Southern Italians illustrate gesturally the
'objects' of their mental acts, the East European ghetto Jews character-

istically produce a gestural notation for the 'process' of their mental activity. This is not a kind of visual representation but a kind of musical scoring. The traditional Jews studied by Efron very rarely employed their hands and arms in the form of a pencil or brush to depict the 'things' to which they referred. They used their hands and arms, rather, as a baton, to link one proposition to another, to trace the path of a logical journey, and to orchestrate the tempo of their mental movement. The gestures cannot be itemised as 'saying' something; they communicate only to someone who understands the accompanying words, particularly if they are familiar with the meanings of certain stereotyped intonational forms characteristic of Yiddish. Accordingly, when several prominent Jewish actors in New York assisted Efron in his investigations, they were not able, like their Italian counterparts, to create any significant pantomime based on 'Jewish' gestures. For what is produced by these gestural forms is not a pictorial representation of their discourse but an orchestration of it. Almost every gestural inflection corresponds to and acts out a change in logical emphasis, a shift in the direction, or an alteration in the tempo, of thought. These inflections are logical movements, charting the 'high' and 'low', the 'detours' and 'crossroads', of an ideational route. Pressed to its extreme, the logical character of this type of gesture – which cannot be observed in the behaviour of the traditional Southern Italian – becomes most evident at those moments when the movement assumes a quasi-syllogistic form, the bodily inflections corresponding to, embodying, the two premises and the conclusion of the thought pattern.

Efron is thus able to distinguish two classes of gestures. In one type the meaning of the gesture is referential. These gestures may be referential in different ways. The movements of hand, arm and head may refer by means of a sign to a visually present object by actually pointing to it; the movement may depict the form of a visual object, a spatial relationship, or a bodily action; or again the movement may represent either a visual or a logical object by means of a pictorial or a non-pictorial form which has no morphological relationship to the thing represented. All these are varieties of a single basic type: referential gesture. They may be contrasted with a second type in which the meaning of the gesture is notational. These movements have meaning because of the structuring and emphasis they provide for the content of the verbal discourse that accompanies them; they enact bodily the pauses, intensities and inflections of the corresponding speech sequence; they trace in the air the directions taken by a flight of thought. This type of movement is a gestural portrayal, not of the 'thought' or 'object' of reference, but of the felt course of the ideational process.

Given this distinction, we may say that both the Southern Italian and the

81

East European Jew 'talk with their hands', but this is literally true of the former and metaphorically true of the latter. On the one hand, gestural onomatopoeia (depicting the form of an object, a spatial relationship, or a bodily action) and gestural emblems (representing a visual or logical object by a pictorial or non-pictorial movement which is not morphologically related to the referent) are frequently encountered in the behaviour of the Southern Italian and rarely met with in that of the Eastern Jew. On the other hand, notational gestures (delineating the course of a thought process), so typical of the Eastern Jew, are virtually unobservable in the Southern Italian. The availability of particular gestural repertoires in the hand movements of individuals of either group depends largely on their history, their cultural belongingness; and the appropriate performance of the movements drawn from the repertory both depends upon the habit memory of their members and tacitly recalls their memory of that communal allegiance.

As an example of *proprieties* of the body we might consider table manners. The topic is addressed in explicit detail in a famous treatise by Erasmus, his *De civilitate morum puerilium* of 1530.[14] This book specifies maxims of conduct with respect to what Erasmus calls 'outward bodily propriety'; such 'outward' proprieties, of bodily carriage, gesture, posture, facial expression and dress, being seen as the expression of the 'inner' person. The impact of the treatise was immediate, wide and lasting. In the first six years after its publication it was reprinted more than thirty times; it was rapidly translated into English, French and German; and in all there were more than 130 editions, thirteen of these as late as the eighteenth century. The questions addressed in this treatise, like those treated in Castiglione's *Il Cortegiano* and Della Casa's *Galateo*, gave new precision and centrality to the concept of *civilitas*, variously rendered as the French *civilité*, the English *civility*, and the Italian *civiltà*. Since decorum and restraint were essential attributes of civility, it was natural that crucial importance should be assigned to the cultured control of appetite in the most literal sense, and hence to table manners.

Some people, says Erasmus, devour food rather than eat it. They behave as if they were thieves wolfing down their booty or as if they were about to be carried off to prison. They put their hands into the dishes when they are scarcely seated and push so much into their mouths at once that their cheeks bulge like bellows. They eat and drink without even pausing, not because they are hungry or thirsty, but because they can control their movements in no other way. They scratch their heads or play with a knife or are unable to refrain from coughing and snorting and spitting. All such signs of rustic embarrassment and coarseness must be avoided. You should not be the first to take food from a dish. You should not search the whole dish with your hand or turn the dish around so that a better piece comes to you, but should simply take the first piece that presents itself. It is impolite to lick greasy fingers or to dip bread you have already bitten into the sauce. It is indecorous to offer someone else some of the meat you are eating and it shows a want of elegance to remove chewed food from the mouth and put it back on the plate. And it is good if conversation interrupts the meal from time to time.

In *The Civilizing Process* Norbert Elias fastens upon Erasmus' text, among others, in the course of demonstrating that nothing in modern Western table manners is self-evident or the expression of a 'natural' feeling of delicacy or simply 'reasonable'; if they have become all that, it is by virtue of being a set of particular practices built up slowly in a historical process of long duration.[15] The implements used at the Western table are not implements with obvious purposes and evident usages. Over the course of centuries, and particularly between the sixteenth and eighteenth centuries, their functions were gradually defined, their forms consolidated, and the values attached to those functions and forms slowly inculcated. The way in which knife, fork and spoon are held and moved was standardised step by step; the practice of using a fork was acquired slowly, as was the habit of taking liquid only with a spoon. By the end of the eighteenth century the French leisured upper class had fully elaborated the standard of table manners that came gradually to be seen as self-evident in Western civilised society as a whole. The shapes of eating utensils are from then on no more than variations on accomplished themes, and the method of handling them remains from that time on unchanged in its essential features. These are a set of historically specific proprieties of the body; they are technical skills imbued with moral values. They are 'forgotten' as maxims only when they have been well remembered as habits.

What is being remembered is a set of rules for defining 'proper' behaviour; the control of appetite in the most literal sense is part of a much wider process which will appear, depending upon our vantage point, either as a structure of feeling or as a pattern of institutional control. These vantage points are reciprocally enlightening since the whole process has to be understood as occurring at two interlocking levels. There is the formation of a type of person whose sensibility is attuned to the more exacting and meticulous promptings of decorum; and there is the formation of a type of society whose control over its members is more stratified and more centralised. At one level there is a particularly strong development of individual self-control. Rules of etiquette impose internalised restraints upon any indiscriminate display of feeling, and teach attentiveness to the finer nuances of propriety and to the distinctions between public and private life. At another level there is a particularly marked development of social control. Rules of court society impose a well-regulated social distance between classes of people who are distinguishable by publicly observable standards of refined behaviour. The social control which is the prerogative of court society and the self-control which is the attainment of a 'civilised' person are mutually defining. It is the merit of Elias to have seized upon this concomitance, to have shown that what is analytically separable is historically inextricable.

The body is the point of linkage between these two levels. It is in bodily proprieties that the rules of etiquette and the rules of the court are reproduced and remembered. They are remembered as habit-memories, as habitually observed rules of decorum. Decorum enjoins that appetite must be satisfied in appropriate form, especially in the incorporating act par excellence, consumption. The precarious sway of culture over nature is celebrated by making the meal an occasion for the demonstration of taste. This, as Bourdieu reminds us, is a way of denying the primary function of consumption, which is to satisfy a common need, by making the meal an occasion for the celebration of artistic refinement and ethical value.[16] There is a studied commitment to stylisation: in the etiquette governing the use of utensils, the seating plan, the sequence of the meal, in the proprieties observed for serving others and oneself, waiting until the last person served has begun to eat, taking modest helpings, not appearing too eager, and in the tacit censorship of noise and haste which would make too crudely blatant the bodily manifestations of the pleasure in eating. This commitment to stylisation moves the focus of attention from substance and function to form and manner, and by doing so tends to deny the crudely material reality of the things consumed and the act of eating them. Just as the capitalist class were to veil the socially organised system of production which underlay and potentiated the circulation of commodities, so the leisured courtly class veiled the material reality of the act of consumption which underlay and potentiated the circulation of civilities. This masking required a mnemonics of the body.

As regards *ceremonies* of the body, we may consider those practices through which the French nobility of the seventeenth century displayed their privileged status. Systematically in the *Projets de Gouvernement du duc de Bourgogne* of 1714–15, and anecdotally in the *Mémoires*, the Comte de Saint-Simon gives us a picture of the French society of his time.[17] This was a society of strictly graded 'orders' or 'estates', a hierarchy of dignities and qualities marked out by the rigorous observance of titles, ranks and symbols. Saint-Simon gives long and minute prescriptions about ceremonial behaviour: about who must have 'the hand', that is to say the right, in certain situations, about the places of honour, the use of carriages, the bearing of arms, the wearing of costumes. These prescriptions serve a polemic end. The goal of the *Projets* was avowedly reactionary. In the society of orders and estates, the greatest honour, until the sixteenth century, had been attributed to the profession of arms. But gradually, at least since the reign of Henry IV, the profession of magistrate had begun to receive as much honour as the bearing of arms; the robe became the social equal of the sword. And under Louis XIV many others were ennobled through the exercise of their profession: men of letters, painters, sculptors, architects, doctors, surgeons, chemists, botanists, even the dignity of commerce was acknowledged. Saint-Simon hated this 'reign of the vile bourgeoisie' and the process of 'mechanical ennoblement'. Ennoblement, he argued, should be allowed only for deeds of arms and long military service. The idea of honour as the principle of social classification should be reaffirmed, and this was to be done by re-establishing the essentially military character of the nobility.

Social stratification by 'order', subdivided into 'estates', consisted of a hierarchy of degrees, each one distinct from the other, and organised according to the honour, the rank and esteem attributed to social functions that could have no connection with the production of material goods.[18] All writers agree that nobility is a quality inherent in the person, and seventeenth-century writers, in particular, insist on the quality of hereditary transmission. To be presented at court it was necessary, in principle, to belong to the ancient nobility. From 1732 it was necessary to prove three hundred years of military nobility without known beginning; a ruling of 1760 required that for such a privilege one should belong to a family traceable as noble back before 1400. Genealogies, which taught the true social position of people, the reasons for which they had allied or misallied themselves with this family or that, were highly prized. Saint-Simon, somewhat scornfully, wishing to show that Louis XIV betrayed an ignorance which 'sometimes made him fall, in public, into the most gross absurdities', gives of this ignorance two examples, which are that the king, not knowing either that Renel belonged to the family of Clermont-Gallerande or that Saint-Herem belonged to that of Montmorin, treated these two men as though they were of low extraction, and that, even when disabused of his error with respect to Saint-Herem, it still had to be explained to him 'what these houses were, for their names conveyed nothing to him'.[19] La Roque, more piously, said that 'every man who is the issue of great and illustrious persons senses always in the depths of his heart a certain impulse which urges him to imitate them: and their memory incites him to glory and fine deeds'.[20] La Bruyère, more wryly, said that a man about court, if he wished to sustain credulity in the rank he claimed for himself, 'must talk to all and sundry about my line, my branch, my name, my coat of arms'.[21] The genealogy might be fabricated; but noble privileges were ceremonially referred to ancestors whose achievements and merits were held to have endured in the blood. Nothing demonstrates more evidently the extent to which it was necessary, in a society of estates, to claim honour, not by reference to the usefulness of functions performed, but by explicit reference to the memory, or at least the ostensible memory, of society.

My lineage, my branch, my name, my coat of arms: all these terms, while insistently referring to the qualities inherent in the possessor, express those qualities in an idealised form; they allude in a somewhat etherealised manner to something that is distinctly and directly corporeal: blood. The value of blood is that of a sign; one may say of one's ancestors that they have shed it in a certain way and of oneself that one is of the same blood. The differentiation into orders and estates, the system of marriage alliances, the value of a noble descent – all show that the blood relation is crucial in the mechanisms and ceremonies of power. Here, as Foucault says, power speaks *through* blood; it is a reality with a symbolic function.[22] The true nobility is a race. But if blood proves membership of an ancient group, that membership must also be visibly displayed. It is displayed through ceremonial privileges and through ceremonial avocations.

Life at the French court was built around ceremonies of privilege. Its daily routine followed a fixed public sequence.[23] This began with the royal *lever* during which the king said his prayers in public; he was dressed in public, he walked to Mass attended by courtiers, he dined in public, he admitted certain courtiers to his leisure activities at the hunt or visiting stables and gardens, he welcomed the whole court to more formal evening entertainments, he ended the day publicly with the royal *coucher*. This daily ceremonial sequence was set apart from the king's directly political work as a ruler, his attendance at council meetings and his discussion with individual ministers. The group of courtiers did not advise the king as ruler; the formal display of their presence at Court bore ceremonial witness to the order of a blood-tie which linked his right to rule and their right to rank. Their uniquely social pre-eminence was attested by numerous privileges. To be part of the daily routine of the king's *lever* and *coucher*, to wait on him at table, to play billiards with him, to accompany him hunting or during his walks in the grounds at Versailles, were highly valued honours. It was an honour too to attend the evening entertainments, the *apartements*, which took place several times a week, with music, dancing, card-playing and buffets. Greater honours still were reserved for a more restricted blood group at court, the *ducs et pairs*. They alone were allowed to enter the courts of the royal palaces on horseback or in carriages; they had precedence immediately after the princes of the blood at baptism, marriages, funerals, and royal banquets; in the marriage contracts of royal children they signed after princes of the blood; they were addressed as 'cousin' by the king and had the right of the honourable epithets of 'Monseigneur' and 'Votre Grandeur'; they alone could wear the ducal crown and the ducal coat; they entered the *parlement* wearing swords, were seated in raised positions, were the first to be allowed to speak. These ceremonial privileges were a mnemonics of the body, a constant reminder of the order of estates.

Ceremonial avocations, no less than ceremonial privileges, display membership of an ancient group. These avocations represent an investment of time and skill in a particular type of symbolic capital: the objects endowed with the greatest symbolic power are those which display the quality inherent in the possessor by clearly demonstrating the quality required in their appropriation.[24] Objects of symbolic, as distinct from financial, capital are as it were locked into the whole life history, and therefore the memories, of those who possess them. For part of the point of what is possessed is precisely that it cannot be managed by leading a life independently of the specific demands of what is possessed. And part of the point of what is possessed is that it is not independent of the past context in which it was acquired. Objects attesting to nobility must be objects which cannot be acquired either by proxy or in haste. To own a chateau or manor house is not primarily to display disposal over money; one must appropriate also the skill of bottling and tasting fine wines, the secrets of fishing, the skills of gardening, the knowledge of the hunt. All these competences are ancient, they can be learned only slowly, they can be enjoyed only by those who take their time, they manifest a concern for things that last. These require that one occupy one's time not economically but ceremonially. Ceremonial avocations, less formally but no less evidently than ceremonial privileges, affirm the principle of hereditary transmission.

Ceremonies, proprieties and techniques of the body exist along a spectrum of possibilities extending from the more or less formal to the more or less informal. All in varying ways entail cognitive memory. Thus ceremonies of the body, such as are exemplified in court etiquette at Versailles, remind performers of a system of honour and hereditary transmission as the organising principle of social classification. Blood relations are signs cognitively known and recalled through the visibly elaborate display of privileges and avocations which make sense only by constant reference to that principle. The ceremonial display of presence at court here establishes a relationship between the organisation of courtly space and the stratification of social relations, behaviour in courtly space being both a form of cultural representation and a mnemonic system. Again, proprieties of the body, such as those illustrated in the development of table manners in early modern Europe, remind performers of a set of rules for defining 'proper' behaviour and for the control of appetite, where the category of appetite is to be understood both literally and by metaphorical extension to a whole structure of individual sensibility and institutional control. Rules of stylisation deny the crudely material reality of the things consumed and the act of consuming them. These rules of proper style express through performance a socially and historically specific distinction between civilisation and nature. Finally, techniques of the body, such as those exemplified by the gestural behaviour of the traditional Southern Italian, would not be possible without the performers' cognitive memory of a communal lexicon. This gestural vocabulary, comprising at least a hundred and fifty items, is a referential system. The very things and notions referred to by the accompanying words are illustrated through a repertoire of movements automatically performed.

In each of these cases, performers are reminded of something with cognitive content. But in each case, too, it is through the act of performance that they are reminded of it. Bodily practices of a culturally specific kind entail a combination of cognitive and habit-memory. The appropriate performance of the movements contained in the repertoire of the group not only reminds the performers of systems of classification which the group holds to be important; it requires also the exercise of habit-memory. In the performances explicit classifications and maxims tend to be taken for granted to the extent that they have been remembered as habits. Indeed, it is precisely because what is performed is something to which the performers are habituated that the cognitive content of what the group remembers in common exercises such persuasive and persistent force.

3

It is not enough to chart the range and itemise the types of behaviour that fall under the category of incorporated practices; we need also to see precisely how these practices are incorporated, that is to say, we need to seize on their habitual quality.

Consider the behaviour of Proust's Saint-Loup, as observed by the narrator Marcel:

On the other hand there were moments when my mind distinguished in Saint-Loup a personality more generalised than his own, that of the 'nobleman', which like an indwelling spirit moved his limbs, ordered his gestures and his actions; then, at such moments, although in his company, I was alone, as I should have been in front of a landscape the harmony of which I could understand. He was no more than an object the properties of which, in my musing, I sought to explore. The discovery in him of this pre-existent, this immemorial being, this aristocrat who was precisely what Robert aspired not to be, gave me intense joy, but a joy of the mind rather than the feelings. In the moral and physical agility which gave so much grace to his kindnesses, in the ease with which he offered my grandmother his carriage and helped her into it, in the alacrity with which he sprang from the box when he was afraid that I might be cold, to spread his own cloak over my shoulders, I sensed not only the inherited litheness of the mighty hunters who had been for generations the ancestors of this young man who had no pretensions except to intellectuality, their scorn of wealth which, subsisting in him side by side with his enjoyment of it simply because it enabled him to entertain his friends more lavishly, made him so carelessly shower his riches at their feet; I sensed in it above all the certainty or the illusion in the minds of those great lords of being 'better than other people', thanks to which they had not been able to hand down to Saint-Loup that anxiety to show that one is 'just as good as the next man', the dread of seeming too assiduous of which he was indeed wholly innocent and which mars with so much stiffness and awkwardness the most sincere plebeian civility.[25]

Even if we mentally subtract from this description the social snobbery animating it and the theory of inherited characteristics embedded within it, and by relegating these aspects of encomium and explanation consider the passage as far as possible strictly as description, the reader will surely feel that it contains an element that is both precise and just. The feature of the passage on which I wish to focus is the embodied character of the object described. Most of the items of behaviour and qualities of character singled out for praise are presented either directly in terms of particular forms of bodily movement and expression, or else in ways that would usually be at least partially identified by means of such bodily expressions. Thus something 'like an indwelling spirit moved his limbs', and 'ordered his gestures and his actions', showing itself in 'moral and physical agility', in kindness infused with 'grace', in help offered with 'ease' and 'alacrity'; and this entire accomplishment of 'ease' and 'litheness' prompts the spectator, Marcel, to contrast it with the 'stiffness' and 'awkwardness' which he observes in what he calls 'plebeian civility'. The accumulated words and phrases are drawn mainly from the impressions which Marcel forms of Saint-Loup in the context of his bodily presence.

Saint-Loup's behaviour impresses Marcel not only by virtue of the qualities rendered transparent through it; what brings Marcel to remark particularly on those qualities is the fact that Saint-Loup consciously wishes to disown certain characteristics of the aristocrat's life. Proust shows us that this conscious disowning is belied by the primary impression. The impressiveness of the effect created by Saint-Loup's behaviour resides at least in part in the contrast between a notion of behaviour ('the aristocrat who was precisely what Robert aspired not to be') and the behaviour itself (where the 'nobleman' in Saint-Loup 'like an indwelling spirit moved his limbs, ordered his gestures and his actions'). This contrast between a notion and a practice of behaviour appears in the form of a contrast between an 'ease' that is 'natural' and an 'ease' that is 'forced'. The ease that is called natural is perceived as natural because of its spontaneous casualness of manner and its even flow of performance. The ease that is called forced is perceived as forced because of the evident presence in that behaviour which intends to display ease of 'false notes', mere signs of a manner of behaving: an anxious reference to what is considered a legitimate norm, an uneasiness about the correct manner to adopt, a respect for a cultural code that is recognised rather than known. The point of remarking upon the contrast between an ease of manner that is called natural and an ease of manner that is called forced is that this contrast cannot be appropriately expressed by saying that the two types of behaviour obey two different codes, or by saying that one type obeys an elaborated while the other obeys a restricted code of behaviour. Marcel's observation of Saint-Loup's behaviour shows us that no notion of a code of bodily performances, however elaborated that code is imagined to be, can comprehend the object described when the object described is a practice of bodily behaviour. For the essential distinction Proust is making here refers not to the range of possibilities made potentially available by the code in question, but rather to the quite different contrast between being able to *recognise* a code and being able to *incorporate* it.[26] Proust's description reminds us that we judge a code of bodily practice to be merely recognised, or alternatively to be incorporated, primarily from the impressions we form of people by virtue of their bodily presence and actions. The impressions created by physical conformation and bodily carriage are those manifestations of the person least susceptible to willed modification, and it is for this reason that they are held to signify the habitual 'nature' of the person.

Saint-Loup's ease arises from the assurance that he is able to embody the socially legitimate body and so is able to impose the norms by which his own body is perceived and accepted by others. It is the body of one who has the habit of ruling. That is why political disputes so frequently resort to visual caricature, in which the body-image of the rulers is physically distorted; caricature deforms in order to ridicule the imposition of an embodied authority. It is a version of such embodied authority which Saint-Loup incarnates, not by mechanically executing codes or punctiliously applying rules, which would have blemished the exemplary effect, but by the prestigious ease of his practised performance. The counter-pole to Saint-Loup's ease is petit-bourgeois embarrassment. This arises from the continual feeling of a gap between the socially legitimate body and the body which one has and is. Unable to incarnate an acknowledged model, one tries vainly to compensate for this inability through the proliferation of the signs of bodily control. This is why the petit-bourgeois experience of the world is characterised by timidity and unease: the unease of those who feel that their bodies betray them and who regard their bodies, as it were, from the outside and through the appraising eyes of others, surveying and correcting their practices. This too is a habit of performance; but it is a habitual experience of the body as a condition of unease, as a perpetual source of awkwardness, as the all too tangible occasion for experiencing a fissure between the body one might wish to have and the body one sees in the mirror: a fissure of which one is being perpetually reminded both by the reactions of others and by the process of self-monitoring by which they notice and try to rectify the gap between the socially legitimate body and the body one has.

Consider now a passage in which the difficulties of someone at an early stage of learning to play jazz on the piano are described:

The music was not mine. It was going on all around me. I was in the midst of the music like a lost newcomer who finds himself suddenly in the midst of a Mexico City traffic circle, but with no particular humor in the situation . . . I started going up with a fast, sputtering, and nervous scale course, and the next chord came up and I had to shoot back down to the middle of the keyboard, to get the thing I knew how to do well done for it, and then there was the next chord. My hand jumped around from place to place like Chaplin stabbing about with his wrenches . . . My looking was occasionally needed to keep the terrain under regard, to aid large leaps necessary to get from one part onto another, a looking that felt frantic, like search-ing for a parking place in a big hurry. The music was literally out of hand.[27]

This is one of many passages in which David Sudnow analyses his at-tempts over five years to play jazz, in the course of which he had many occasions to meditate on the failures in what he calls, in a fine phrase, the management of improvised conduct. By observing the minutiae of his body's movements he shows how a whole variety of expanding skills, co-ordinated ways of looking, moving, reaching, thinking, have to be developed if one is to be able to execute correct successions of chords. For imagine this single item in the repertoire: Here are chord A and chord B, separated by some distance along the keyboard. To play A you must have a tightly compressed hand; to play B you need an extended spread of the hand. To play A you must align your body with the keyboard in the way you come at a typewriter to establish contact with the home position. To play B you must adjust the axis of your hand relative to the keyboard, the little finger reaching further away from the body's centre than the thumb. The distance between A and B cannot just be crossed; it must be spontaneously traversed in a specific manner. If you are to go correctly from A to B, your hand, indeed your whole body, must be directed from the start not just toward where B is; your hand must be preparing along the course of your journey to land in the right productional shape as it arrives at B in correct tempo. As your hand moves from A toward B a smooth course of changing hand shape must be accomplished; all the necessary minute adjustments have to occur spontaneously and simultaneously in the appropriate reconfiguration of your hand and in a slight readjustment of your body.

Beginners get from A to B disjointedly. They play A, and set out for B without going for it in the right way from the outset, without moving to the whole of B and in correct tempo. Before they have become skilled in playing scales, beginners hunt and peck at the keyboard, their fingers hesitate and lose their place. They continually sense a separation between the 'it' of the piano and the 'me' of the pianist. A more advanced pianist, playing a rapid and intricately winding passage and its reiteration, will frequently come close but slightly miss the mark; will have a sense of 'struggling to make it happen' and will 'sound like someone trying hard to say something'. Sudnow suggests a number of analogies for this experience of disjointedness. Failed improvisations are undermined in the same way as when one first gets the knack of a complex skill, like riding a bicycle or skiing; the attempt to sustain an easy management of the skill breaks down and 'you struggle to stay balanced, keep falling, and then almost suddenly several revolutions of the pedals are sustained with the bicycle seeming to go off on its own, and you try to keep it up, and it disintegrates'. These attempted improvisations recall the confusions of Charlie Chaplin on the assembly line in *Modern Times*. The conveyor belt continuously carries a ceaseless collection of nuts and bolts to be tightened; Chaplin holds two wrenches in his hands, falls behind time, rushes to catch up, screws nuts and bolts faster still in an effort to keep ahead, misses one or two because he has become frantic, gets ejected through a corridor in a jerky dance. Or again, the difference between disjointedly trying to play jazz and catching on to what successful playing feels like, is similar to the difference between 'the aphasic's or stutterer's or brain-damaged speaker's or new foreigner's attempts' to construct a smooth sentence, and 'the competent three year-old's flowing utterance'.

What does it mean to achieve this flowing utterance? It means that the process of looking for notes, the explicit seeking and finding of recognisable and visually grasped places out there, has become redundant. It means that one has acquired, from a habitual position at the middle of the piano, an incorporated sense of places and distances and pressures. To be able to sit at a piano and get an initial orientation by the slightest touch 'anywhere' on the keyboard; to bring your finger precisely to a spot 'two feet' to your left, where half an inch off or a different pressure on arrival would have been a mistake; to move another 'seventeen inches' and strike another note just as precisely; to move another 'twenty-three inches' just as accurately; to execute all these moves rapidly and spontaneously as when, if ordered to touch your ear or your knee, you move your hand to your ear or your knee by the shortest route and without having to think of the initial position of your hand, or that of your ear, or the path between them; to be as familiar with a terrain of hands and keyboard whose respective surfaces have become as intimately known as the respective surfaces of your tongue and teeth and palate: to do all this, which is to master a range of skills any competent jazz player has at his command, is to have a habitual knowledge – one might equally say a remembrance – in the hands; it is to have, as Sudnow puts it, 'an embodied way of accomplishing distances' which can be accomplished only through 'a long course of incorporation'.[28]

What we have learnt from the examples described by Proust and Sudnow may now be drawn together in certain general propositions about the nature of habit as it affects incorporated practice.

Habits are more than technical abilities. When we think of habitual behaviour in terms of walking and swimming, knitting and typewriting, we tend to think of habits as skills, technical abilities of varying degrees of complexity which are at our disposal but which exist apart from our likes and dislikes and lack any quality of urgency or impulsion or marked affective disposition. We think of them as skills waiting to be called into action on the appropriate occasion. Dewey suggests that if we wish to appreciate the peculiar place and force of habit in our activities we should consider the case of bad habits: an addiction to alcohol and drugs, gambling and idling. When we reflect on such habits we will be impressed by the role played by desire in habitual behaviour. For what we can observe clearly in the case of bad habits is the hold they exert over us, the way in which they impel us toward certain courses of action. These habits entail an inherent tendency to act in a certain way, an impulsion strong enough to lead us habitually to do things which we tell ourselves we would prefer not to do, and to act in ways that belie or override our conscious decisions and formal resolutions. Dewey's point is that this feature is not specific to a particular class of bad habits; these characteristics of bad habits are precisely the features which are most instructive about all habits.[29] They remind us, as Marcel Proust's and David Sudnow's reflections on habitual skills also lead us to see, that all habits are affective dispositions: that a predisposition formed through the frequent repetition of a number of specific acts is an intimate and fundamental part of ourselves, that such habits have power because they are so intimately a part of ourselves.

A habit is more than a disposition. Better than the term disposition, the word habit gives us a way of referring to that kind of activity in which a cluster of features are collected together to form a practice: an activity which is acquired in the sense that it is influenced by previous activity; which is ready for overt manifestation; and which remains operative in some subdued way even when it is not the obviously dominant activity. We might choose the word disposition to express all this, but it would be a little misleading. The term disposition suggests something latent or potential, something which requires a positive stimulus outside ourselves for it to become actively engaged. The term habit conveys the sense of operativeness, of a continuously practised activity. It conveys the fact of exercise, the reinforcing effect of repeated acts. This is the feature of habit that is brought into prominence by considering technical skills whose exercise diminishes the conscious attention with which our acts are performed. When we are learning to walk, to swim, to ride, to skate or to sing, we frequently interrupt ourselves by unnecessary movements and false notes. When we have become proficient the results follow with the minimum of muscular action to bring them about and they flow from a single cue. By exercise the body comes to co-ordinate an increasing range of muscular activities in an increasingly automatic way, until awareness retreats, the movement flows 'involuntarily', and there occurs a firm and practised sequence of acts which take their fluent course. The feats of acrobats and jugglers illustrate an extreme version of this, as also do the prestigious skills described by Proust and Sudnow. But automatic exercise can be banal as well as prestigious and, instead of being smooth and harmonious, it can be habitually clumsy and disharmonious. Patterns of body use become ingrained through our interactions with objects. There are the apparently automatic, long familiar movements of artisans, the way a carpenter wields a plane and the weaver uses a loom, so habitual that, if asked, they would say that they had a feeling of the proper management of the implement in their hands; there are the ways that working at a machine or at a desk imposes and reinforces a set of postural behaviours which we come to regard as 'belonging' to the factory worker or the sedentary white-collar worker. Postures and movements which are habit memories become sedimented into bodily conformation. Actors can mimic the impressions, doctors can examine the results.

Above all, therefore, habit is not just a sign. Embodied experience, of which habitual practices form a significant part, has recently been subjected to a cognitive imperialism and interpreted in terms of a linguistic model of meaning. Society, made in the image and likeness of language, assumes the role of endowing with meaning the physical bodies and behaviours of individuals. The body, reduced to the status of a sign, signifies by virtue of being a highly adaptable vehicle for the expression of mental categories. And metaphors of bodily activity, like 'falling', are seen as expressing a concept in terms of a bodily image. This is to view understanding as a process in which a sense-datum is subsumed under an idea, and to view the body as an object arbitrarily carrying meanings. But, as Merleau-Ponty has rightly remarked, the phenomenon of habit should prompt us to revise our notion of 'understand' and our notion of the body.[30] To know how to type, for instance, is neither to know the place of each letter among the keys, nor is it to have acquired a conditioned reflex for each letter, which is set in motion by each letter as it comes before the eye. We know where the letters are on the typewriter as we know where one of our limbs is. We remember this through knowledge bred of familiarity in our lived space. The movement of the typist's fingers may be describable; yet it is not present to the typist as a trajectory through space that can be described, but as a certain adjustment of the typist's mobility. Here a meaningful practice does not coincide with a sign; meaning cannot be reduced to a sign which exists on a separate 'level' outside the immediate sphere of the body's acts. Habit is a knowledge and a remembering in the hands and in the body; and in the cultivation of habit it is our body which 'understands'.

4

It has long been acknowledged that both incorporating and inscribing practices may be the objects of our interpretive activity. This acknowledgement dates back at least to Schleiermacher's proposal of a general hermeneutics. Interpretation is now seen as the explicit, conscious understanding of meanings under conditions where an understanding of those meanings can no longer be presumed to be a self-evident process but is viewed instead as intrinsically problematic; it is here assumed that misunderstandings about what we seek to interpret will arise not occasionally but systematically. Nor is our interpretive activity tied to any particular subject-matter; the unity of hermeneutics resides in the unity of a procedure which is applicable to any object and any practice capable of bearing a meaning. Works of art, musical compositions, theatrical performances, ritual acts, coins, prehistoric monuments and implements, bodily expressions, gestures, postures and movements – Schleiermacher's move explicitly makes them all into possible objects of interpretive activity.[31]

Yet although incorporated practices are in principle included as possible objects of hermeneutic inquiry, in practice hermeneutics has taken inscription as its privileged object. Hermeneutics arose out of philology; and throughout its history it has returned to philology, that is, to the kind of relationship with tradition which focusses on the transmission of what has been inscribed, on texts, or, at the very least, on the transmission of documents and monuments to which authority is ascribed because they are held to have a status comparable to texts, to be constituted in the image and likeness of a text. Thus Schleiermacher, who founded a general theory of interpretation, was the exegete of the New Testament and the translator of Plato. Thus Dilthey, who produced a critique of historical reason, located the specificity of interpretation (*Auslegung*) as contrasted with direct understanding (*Verstehen*) in the phenomenon of fixation by writing and, more generally, inscription. Thus Ricoeur, who insists on the centrality of hermeneutics for the human sciences as a whole, remarks also on the peculiar character of the work that is written, to which traditional hermeneutics ascribed the authority of model, as lying in its capacity to transcend the social conditions of its production and reception, and thus to open itself to a potentially unlimited series of socially situated readings.[32]

Inscriptions, and hence texts, were privileged objects of interpretation because the activity of interpretation itself became an object of reflection, rather than being simply practised, in a particular context. As a cumulative process, reflection on the practice of interpretation arose in modern European culture as a result of the attempt to understand what had been handed down within that culture from the past; only secondarily and subsequently did the activity of interpretation appear problematic in the form of attempts to understand geographically distant non-European cultures. An explicit awareness that we can hand on a tradition only if we can interpret a tradition took shape when the practice of handing on the traditional substance of European culture ceased to be self-evident and became an occasion of systematic misunderstanding. But that occurred because this substance had a certain form. What is handed down in the form of a text within a single culture is transmitted like nothing else that comes down to us from the past in that culture. Detached both from its producers and from any specific addressees, a text can lead a life of its own; it enjoys relative cultural autonomy. It is the ideality of the word that raises linguistic objects beyond the finiteness and transience of the remnants of past existence. What has been fixed in writing enters into a sphere of publicly accessible meanings in which everyone who can subsequently read that writing has potentially a share in its meanings.

This is preeminently the case with respect to two types of text in particular. Jurisprudence and theology are essentially hermeneutic procedures because both depend on the exegesis of written statements. Legal hermeneutics is concerned with interpreting principles of behaviour which have to be observed as criteria for evaluating social behaviour within the framework of a valid legal order. Theological hermeneutics is a form of interpretation whose principles and limits are prescribed by a holy written text and by the way in which the interpreter of that text is bound by the confession of a system of religious beliefs. In both cases, in legal as in theological interpretation, application is an integral element of understanding. In legal as in theological hermeneutics there is a tension between, on the one hand, the text that has been set down, whether legal statute or religious proclamation, and, on the other hand, the sense that is arrived at by applying that text in the particular present moment of interpretation, whether in legal judgement or in preaching and liturgy. Neither a legal system nor a religious proclamation can be understood purely as historical documents. A legal system has to be made concretely valid in the present by being interpreted. A religious proclamation in the very process of being proclaimed is held to exercise a saving effect. In both cases the act of interpretation is in principle normative; in both cases the process of understanding is an act of application.[33]

More specifically still, two texts have figured largely in the history of hermeneutics, Roman Law and Holy Scripture, and the changing fate of interpretation in both cases has been strikingly analogous. Roman Law as it was known from the Codification of Justinian had authority as a binding set of legal propositions for nearly a thousand years.[34] Particularly in the late Middle Ages, secular legal science was almost entirely focussed on the exegesis of Roman Law; at Bologna its components were collated and organised into a text that remained until the sixteenth century the standard edition of the *Corpus Juris*; and it was through the study of this text that Roman concepts were adapted to the needs of medieval Europe. But this process of assimilation depended on premises that were never systematically examined. It was assumed that the Roman Law of the later Empire was a perfect system, a self-contained and internally consistent whole, the rules of which were valid universally. And it was assumed that the Roman Law as it was taught to medieval jurists was identical with the law of Rome as it was understood by Justinian. These premises rested, in turn, on a certain idea of Rome. The glossators believed that the 'Imperium Romanum' of Justinian had never disappeared; his legislation was thought to have continued directly in existence in the Christian Empire and to be still valid. Because of the supposed metaphysical identity of the *Corpus Christianum* and the Roman Empire, it was thought that the world in which people lived was still legally the same as that of the ancient empire.

These assumptions were undermined by the work of the legal humanists.[35] Impressed by the authority of Roman Law, they wanted to recover the exact original meaning of its legal texts. To do this, they set out to rediscover the precise meanings of all the technical and obscure words contained in the texts, by establishing the various meanings which these words possessed in ancient legal texts and in other works of antiquity. The original Justinian text, they discovered, was barnacled by accretions. It had become doubly defaced. It was distorted by the original Byzantine compilers, who had abridged the classical texts and altered them without acknowledgement. And it was distorted by subsequent scholastic commentators, who had further obscured the original structure of the corpus by their elaborate glosses. The effect of philological purification was to reverse the intention animating it. Meaning at the outset to improve Roman Law jurisprudence, the humanists ended by undermining the premises on which it had rested. This result had a negative and a positive aspect. Negatively, it led the legal humanists to the conclusion that the Codification of Justinian was neither perfect nor complete. They found, on the contrary, that much of Roman legal practice had been either omitted or imperfectly recorded in it; that what was included was frequently incoherent; and that many of these loosely assembled enactments referred to the specific requirements of ancient Rome and had little bearing on the different legal conditions of contemporary Europe. Positively, this led the legal humanists to reconstruct the civilisation of ancient Rome historically, as a culture wholly separate from their own. The system of Roman Law was sufficiently comprehensive to provide a detailed and systematic description of the main institutions and ideas of the society of which it formed so significant a part; it was not possible to translate the language of Roman Law back into its original meanings without also reconstructing a picture of Imperial Roman society as a whole. The closeness of philological attention which they brought to its texts increased their sense of historical distance from those texts.

The history of theological interpretation executed a parallel trajectory. Here too a canonic text enjoyed authority over a long period.[36] Jerome's Latin translation of Scripture, dating from about 400, was the authoritative Bible of the Western church throughout the Middle Ages. Nearly all biblical commentaries were based on this Latin text without regard to the wording in the original languages, and whenever a translation into the vernacular was made this text served as the original. The longevity of the authority rested on the premise that it was a faithful, final and sacred reproduction of Holy Writ that must not be changed. This official version of the Bible was esteemed in the knowledge that fathers and forefathers had read and spoken the same words as did subsequent generations. Living languages might change, but the stability of religious belief demanded that the wording of Holy Writ be permanent. The archaic language might cause single words or even complete passages to be no longer fully understood, but reassurance stemmed from the thought that life was lived, as it were, in quotation. The resultant hostility to any attempt to change the text of the Vulgate received reinforcement from the way in which medieval interpretation was assimilated into the study of the text. Great exegetic edifices brought all the sayings of the Bible and all the different interpretations of the Fathers of the Church into agreement. The commentated Latin Bible published in Basle in 1498 and republished in 1502 illustrates the procedure. Even the layout of its pages reveals the operative principle. In the middle of each page there is the text of the Bible in large letters. Between the lines the interlinear gloss is printed in small letters. The commentaries, frequently occupying more space than the passages they interpret, are printed in closest proximity to the biblical text. The text is meant to be read in accordance with the tradition of exegesis which encloses the official Latin version of the Bible.

This premise was undermined by the philology of the humanists, who aimed to recover the exact historical context for the biblical texts and produced new and more precise translations of the ancient Greek and Hebrew writings.[37] Valla announced that philologists could pronounce on doctrinal matters, since no one was entitled to interpret the Bible unless they could read it in the original Hebrew or Greek. Reuchlin discussed the words of Scripture as a grammarian, proposing a method of reading which traced the meaning of every word in the original Hebrew. Erasmus produced a version of the Bible in which the Greek text was printed side by side with his new translation, and in which he explained in annotations at the end precisely where and why his version rejected the text of the Vulgate. The more detailed knowledge of the New Testament that emerged from all this activity undermined the authority of the Vulgate and questioned the role of the Church. The Vulgate was undermined since many previous assumptions about the history of scriptural documents, for example, about their authorship, were shown to be inventions, and since the philologists could demonstrate the inaccuracy of the text on which medieval commentaries had relied. The Church was questioned because the biblical view of the world came to be seen as very different from the world of those who commented on it; and because the contemporary organisation and claims of the Papacy came to be seen as seriously at odds with the original institutions and ideals of the early Church.

Two homologous processes occurred in the study of Roman Law and the Bible. These processes arose from a similar intention and arrived at a comparable result. Medieval and humanist interpreters were alike in accepting antiquity as a model and a norm, in accepting its teachings and canons as authoritative. Where they differed was in the methods chosen to understand antiquity. Medieval interpreters adopted a method of assimilation, synthesis and allegory. They felt no need to distinguish text and commentary, to investigate the way in which the life of the past differed from that of the present, or to establish a systematic method which would enable them to do so. Instead, they adopted what Panofsky has called 'a principle of disjunction': a disjunction between the employment of classical forms and the insistence that these forms carried messages of contemporary significance.[38] This led to an imaginative conflation between the life of antiquity and the life of the contemporary world. The humanist interpreters called for a return to the pure text. This led them to confront a series of problems never considered before in a systematic way. Questions arose concerning the tests of documentary authenticity; the relative authority of different types of texts; the indications of an author's bias; and the logical basis of our beliefs about the past. In dealing with these problems there emerged a method for establishing the authenticity of documents; a definition of the range of sources and a discrimination between original and secondary; criteria for deciding upon the bias of a source; and a formulation of the logical basis of historical belief. Cumulatively, these questions were related together, and led to the formation of a method and theory of historical criticism: an act of critical reading.[39]

This result was paradoxical. The highest aim of the humanists was not originally to 'understand' their models, but to imitate them. For them the word 'classical' expressed a consciousness of something enduring, a sense that the duration of the power of a text to speak directly to subsequent generations was unlimited; and for us too the word 'classical' contains a residue of that meaning. The humanists studied the texts of the ancient world, then, because that world represented for them a norm, something to be copied and imitated. Yet the more accurately and the more thoroughly they pursued their textual studies, the more evident it became that copying and imitation were impossible. The ancient texts, if understood literally, 'as they really were', must be seen as belonging to an ancient world, as bound up with a whole context of meanings that could not be directly assimilated into contemporary culture. Reversing their original intention, the humanists ended by questioning the normative status of their privileged objects. We can express the same process the other way round. What impelled them to establish the foundations of historical discipline – the sense that special techniques were required to investigate the past viewed as an independent field of study without normative claims on the investigator – was the belief that a certain past was normative. This was the dialectic of historical enlightenment: an ironic reversal grounded in the possibilities inherent in inscription.

Inscribing practices have always formed the privileged story, incorporating practices the neglected story, in the history of hermeneutics. The ground was prepared for this backgrounding of bodily practices by modern natural science. The mechanisation of physical reality in the exact natural sciences meant that the body was conceptualised as one object among others in an object-domain made up of moving bodies which obey lawful processes. The body was regarded as a material thing: it was materialised. Bodily practices as such are here lost from view. The response to the mechanisation of physical reality, first in the *Geisteswissenschaften* and later in the 'linguistic turn', reinforced this effect rather than counteracting it. A newly constituted object-domain, the communication of meanings according to rules, could in principle include the body in its domain but did so in practice only peripherally. The object-domain of hermeneutics was defined in terms of what was taken to be the distinctive feature of the human species, first consciousness and later language. When the defining feature was taken to be consciousness, it was acknowledged that the expression of meanings was coupled with human organisms, but in such a coupling nothing more is seen than an empirical fact; the primary objects are canonic texts, and the life of human beings, as a historical life, is understood as a life reported on and narrated, not life as a physical existence. When the defining feature of the human species was seen as language, the body was 'readable' as a text or code, but the body is regarded as the arbitrary bearer of meanings; bodily practices are acknowledged, but in an etherealised form.[40]

There is a good reason why this should have happened. The fact that incorporating practices have for long been backgrounded as objects of explicit interpretive attention is due not so much to a peculiarity of hermeneutics as rather to a defining feature of incorporating practices themselves. For these practices, as we have noted, cannot be well accomplished without a diminution of the conscious attention that is paid to them. The study of habit teaches us this. Any bodily practice, swimming or typing or dancing, requires for its proper execution a whole chain of interconnected acts, and in the early performances of the action the conscious will has to choose each of the successive events that make up the action from a number of wrong alternatives; but habit eventually brings it about that each event precipitates an appropriate successor without an alternative appearing to offer itself and without reference to the conscious will. When we first learn to swim or type or dance we interrupt ourselves at every step by unnecessary movements; when we have become proficient, the results flow with the minimum of muscular action needed to bring them about. Even if the ideational centres are still involved when we successfully perform the chain of acts which together make up the practice, they are involved minimally, as is evident from the fact that our attention may be partly or almost wholly directed elsewhere while accomplishing the practice. The bodily movements are accompanied by sensations, but sensations to which we are normally inattentive; our attention is attracted when they go wrong.

Incorporating practices therefore provide a particularly effective system of mnemonics. In this there is an element of paradox. For it is true that whatever is written, and more generally whatever is inscribed, demonstrates, by the fact of being inscribed, a will to be remembered and reaches as it were its fulfilment in the formation of a canon. It is equally true that incorporating practices, by contrast, are largely traceless and that, as such, they are incapable of providing a means by which any evidence of a will to be remembered can be 'left behind'. In consequence, we commonly consider inscription to be the privileged form for the transmission of a society's memories, and we see the diffusion and elaboration of a society's systems of inscription as making possible an exponential development of its capacity to remember.

Yet it would be misleading, on this account, to underestimate the mnemonic importance and persistence of what is incorporated. Incorporating practices depend for their particular mnemonic effect on two distinctive features: their mode of existence and their mode of acquisition. They do not exist 'objectively', independently of their being performed. And they are acquired in such a way as not to require explicit reflection on their performance. It is important to notice that the relatively informal sets of actions I have referred to as culturally specific bodily practices enjoy significant features in common with the relatively more formal sets of actions I have called commemorative ceremonies. For commemorative ceremonies also are preserved only through their performance; and, because of their performativity and their formalisation, they too are not easily susceptible to critical scrutiny and evaluation by those habituated to their performance. Both commemorative ceremonies and bodily practices therefore contain a measure of insurance against the process of cumulative questioning entailed in all discursive practices. This is the source of their importance and persistence as mnemonic systems. Every group, then, will entrust to bodily automatisms the values and categories which they are most anxious to conserve. They will know how well the past can be kept in mind by a habitual memory sedimented in the body.

There is, then, an inertia in social structures that is not adequately explained by any of the current orthodoxies of what a social structure is. This has implications for social anthropologists, for historians, and for sociologists and social theorists generally.

It has implications for social anthropologists. Not only have I been suggesting that memory, or tradition, gets passed on in non-textual and non-cognitive ways. I am also suggesting that those who have seen the importance of performance, which is (mostly) to say social anthropologists, have emphasised their importance for 'making explicit' the existing social structure; not for emphasising, marking, defining a continuity from the past. Social anthropologists since Malinowski and symbolic anthropologists since Durkheim – witness Lévi-Strauss, in whom the disposition has been reinforced by his addiction to timeless cognitions – have been disinclined to diachrony. Durkheim himself does indeed have a non-cognitive, performative account, in *The Elementary Forms of Religious Life*, of how societies worship themselves, that is, of how they celebrate symbols of themselves in rituals the power of which comes from the emotional effects of social interaction; and this can also serve as an account of what is going on in more distinctively commemorative rituals. This is one instance, one of many, of the fact that some anthropologists have been driving in the same direction as that aimed at in my account; but they have not made the point about commemorations because they have not been interested in the diachronic component of collective identity.

There are implications for those who are pre-eminently concerned with diachrony, that is to say for historians. Historians customarily now insist upon the invention of traditions, and so on the extent to which rituals should be seen as intentional responses to particular and variable social and political contexts. But however invigorating this new historical theme, it cannot be extended indefinitely and without question to explain what is going on in all commemorations. Certainly it is possible to imagine a future in which ceremonies at the Cenotaph no longer take place because there is no generation still alive who can pass on the living memory it recalls; we can envisage a day when such commemorations will have become as meaningless as it already now is for us to commemorate the Battle of Waterloo. But the way in which memory might work in communal celebration is not exhausted by extrapolating from this type of example. The Passover and the Last Supper have for long been remembered without there being any living generation who can, in the above implied sense, remember their originating historical context. The one-sidedness of the approach which insists upon the invention of traditions results from an inability to see the performativity of ritual. The effect is to obscure the distinction between the question of the invention of rituals and the question of their persistence. The historicist demand that we fully review the intentions of the *creators* of a ritual, a demand which in some cases is borrowed explicitly from recent practitioners in the history of ideas, is not only not sufficient but is often not even a necessary condition for understanding ritual. For I would argue that the notion of 'reading' a ritual is here being taken too literally; as a result, the identifying and partially constitutive features of ritual – such as formality and performativity – tend to be largely ignored in the attempt to approximate as closely as possible the interpretation of ritual to that of, say, a literary political tract.

There are implications also for sociologists and social theorists generally. For the dominant mode of self-understanding represented by contemporary conventionalism has, at least until recently, entailed a tendency among social theorists to lose sight of the human body as an object domain. Thus in the case of certain recent conceptions of social theory the object domain for social theory has been defined in terms of what is taken to be the distinctive feature of the human species, language: language itself being conceptualised by the Wittgensteinian, structuralist and poststructuralist schools as a set of social rules, or a system of signs, or a powerful discourse. The human body can be included in an object domain thus defined only as the carrier of linguistic meanings or of meanings structured like a language. It can be included, in other words, only in an etherealised form.

It is true that the body has recently received attention as a bearer of social and political meanings. But even that acknowledgement is cast in an etherealised form. The point is commonly, if not always, made with a markedly cognitive tilt. Frequently what is being talked about is the symbolism of the body or attitudes towards the body or discourses about the body; not so much how bodies are variously constituted and variously behave. It is asserted that the body is socially constituted; but the ambiguity in the term constitution tends to go unexamined. That is to say, the body is seen to be socially constituted in the sense that it is constructed as an object of knowledge or discourse; but the body is not seen equally clearly to be socially constituted in the sense that it is culturally shaped in its actual practices and behaviour. Practices and behaviour are constantly being assimilated to a cognitive model. The ambiguity of meaning in the words constitution and construction tends to be glided over, one of the meanings being privileged at the expense of the other. But the body is socially constituted in a double sense. To argue for the importance of performances, and in particular habitual performances, in conveying and sustaining memory, is, among other things, to insist on that ambiguity and on the significance of the second term of its meaning.

Notes

Introduction

1 Especially in the work of Maurice Halbwachs. See M. Halbwachs, *Les cadres sociaux de la mémoire* (Paris, 1925); *La mémoire collective* (Paris, 1950); *La topographie légendaire des Evangiles en Terre Sainte* (Paris, 1941); 'La mémoire collective chez les musiciens', *Revue Philosophique*, 127 (1939), pp. 136–65. A number of more recent studies should be mentioned in this connection: E. Shils, *Tradition* (London, 1981); Z. Bauman, *Memories of Class* (London, 1982); E. Hobsbawm and T. Ranger (eds.), *The Invention of Tradition* (Cambridge, 1983); P. Nora, *Les lieux de la mémoire* (Paris, 1984); R. Boyers, *Atrocity and Amnesia. The Political Novel since 1945* (Oxford, 1985); B. A. Smith, *Politics and Remembrance* (Princeton, 1985); P. Wright, *On Living in an Old Country* (London, 1985); D. Lowenthal, *The Past is a Foreign Country* (Cambridge, 1985); F. Haug, *Female Sexualization: a Collective Work of Memory* (tr. E. Carter, London, 1987).
2 A valuable corrective to politically sanitizing talk of post-industrialism may be found, for example, in H. Schiller, *Mass Media and American Empire* (New York, 1969); *The Mind Managers* (Boston, 1973); *Communication and Cultural Domination* (New York, 1977); *Information and the Crisis Economy* (Oxford, 1986); but see also A. Mattelart, *Multinational Corporations and the Control of Culture* (tr. M. Chanan, Brighton, 1979).
3 See F. Jameson, *The Political Unconscious* (Ithaca, 1981).
4 M. Proust, *Remembrance of Things Past* (tr. C. K. Scott Moncrieff and T. Kilmartin, London, 1981), vol. I, p. 20.
5 M. Proust, *Remembrance of Things Past*, vol. III, pp. 1007–9.

1   Social memory

1 The terms of this transformation are set out in R. Koselleck, 'Der neuzeitliche Revolutionsbegriff als geschichtliche Kategorie', *Studium Generale*, 22 (1969), pp. 825–38.
2 See T. Schieder, 'Das Problem der Revolution im 19. Jahrhundert', *Historische Zeitschrift*, 170 (1950), p. 233–71; G. Steiner, 'The Great Ennui', in *In*

Bluebeard's Castle: Some Notes Towards the Redefinition of Culture (London, 1971), pp. 11–27.

3 I. Kant, 'Der Streit der Fakultäten' (1778), *Philosophische Bibliothek*, 252, p. 87.

4 On trial by fiat of successor regimes, see O. Kirchheimer, *Political Justice: the Use of Legal Procedure for Political Ends* (Princeton, 1961), pp. 304 ff.

5 A. Camus, *The Rebel* (tr. A. Bower, London, 1953), p. 112.

6 On the distinction between the significance of the private assassination and the public execution of kings see M. Walzer, *Regicide and Revolution* (Cambridge, 1974).

7 On the political theology of kingship see especially E. H. Kantorowicz, *The King's Two Bodies: a Study in Medieval Political Theology* (Princeton, 1957); M. Bloch, *The Royal Touch: Sacred Monarchy and Scrofula in England and France* (tr. J. E. Anderson, London, 1973); L. Hunt, *Politics, Culture, and Class in the French Revolution* (Berkeley, 1984); see also F. Kern, *Kingship and Law in the Middle Ages* (New York, 1970); M. Walzer, *Regicide and Revolution* (Cambridge, 1974).

8 See Walzer, *Regicide and Revolution*, p. 18.

9 On the carnival see M. Bakhtin, *Rabelais and his World* (tr. H. Iswolsky, Cambridge, Mass., 1968), pp. 196–277; and for a more recent exploration of the themes suggested by Bakhtin, P. Stallybrass and A. White, *The Politics and Poetics of Transgression* (London, 1986).

10 For fashions in dress during the French Revolution see Sennett, *The Fall of Public Man* (Cambridge, 1975), pp. 183 ff.

11 See Sennett, *The Fall of Public Man* (Cambridge, 1975), pp. 64–72.

12 M. Oakeshott, *Rationalism in Politics* (London, 1962), p. 119.

13 For a discussion of expectations and genres see especially E. D. Hirsch, *Validity in Interpretation* (New Haven, 1967). A brief treatment of these themes may be found in G. Buck, 'The Structure of Hermeneutic Experience and the Problem of Tradition', *New Literary History*, 10 (1978), pp. 31–48.

14 See R. Collingwood, *The Idea of History* (Oxford, 1946), esp. pp. 266 ff; and J. Goldstein, *Historical Knowledge* (Austin, Texas, 1976), esp. pp. 13–16, 52–9.

15 See F. Gabrieli, 'The Arabic Historiography of the Crusades,' in B. Lewis and P. M. Holt (eds.), *Historians of the Middle East* (London, 1962), pp. 98–107; B. Lewis, *History: Remembered, Recorded, Invented* (Princeton, 1975); E. Sivan, 'Modern Arab Historiography of the Crusades', *Asian and African Studies*, 8 (1972), pp. 102–49.

16 See for example A. Kohli-Kunz, *Erinnern und Vergessen* (Berlin, 1972) and J. Ritter, 'Die Aufgabe der Geisteswissenschaften in der modernen Gesellschaft', *Schriften der Gesellschaft zur Förderung der Westfälischen Wilhelms-Universität zu Münster*, Heft 51 (Münster, 1961).

17 See especially F. Meinecke, *Historism: the Rise of a New Historical Outlook* (tr. J. E. Anderson, London, 1972) and P. H. Reill, *The German Enlightenment and the Rise of Historicism* (Berkeley, 1975); see also I. Berlin, *Vico and*

Herder (London, 1976) and P. Rossi, 'The Ideological Valencies of Twentieth-Century Historicism', *History and Theory*, Beiheft 14 (1975).

18 On role-playing in a society of strangers see R. Sennett, passim.

19 M. Proust, *Remembrance of Things Past* (tr. C. K. Scott Moncrieff and T. Kilmartin, Harmondsworth, 1981), vol. I, p. 62.

20 On gossip in village life see J. Berger, *Pig Earth* (London, 1979). It should be noted, however, that a number of recent studies take it as their task to set the life of villages within a larger social and national context, the economic and political 'outside', the effect of this historical approach being that villages have come to be regarded less as static, isolated entities. See C. Bell and H. Newby, *Community Studies: an Introduction to the Sociology of the Local Community* (London, 1971); J. Boissevain and J. Friedl (eds.), *Beyond Community: Social Process in Europe* (The Hague, 1975); J. Ennew, *The Western Isles Today* (Cambridge, 1980); S. H. Franklin, *Rural Societies* (London, 1971); A. Macfarlane, with S. Harrison and C. Jardine, *Reconstructing Historical Communities* (Cambridge, 1977), on the 'myth of the community'; R. Schulte, 'Village Life in Europe', *Comparative Studies in Society and History*, 27 (1985), pp. 195–206.

21 On the manipulation of political memory through control of records see J. Chesneaux, *Pasts and Futures, or, What is History For?* (London, 1978).

22 See H. Butterfield, *The Discontinuities Between the Generations in History* (Cambridge, 1972).

23 See T. Schieder, 'Das Problem der Revolution im 19. Jahrhundert', *Historische Zeitschrift*, 170 (1950), pp. 233–71.

24 See J. Joll, *1914: The Unspoken Assumptions* (London, 1968).

25 S. Terkel, *Working: people talk about what they do all day and how they feel about what they do* (London, 1975).

26 P. Fussell, *The Great War and Modern Memory* (New York, 1975).

27 C. Levi, *Christ Stopped at Eboli* (tr. F. Frenaye, London, 1963), esp. pp. 130 ff.

28 For a discussion of the narrative accounts embedded in everyday discourse see A. Macintyre, *After Virtue* (London, 1981), pp. 190–201.

29 Mention should be made, however, of a number of recent works which address the question of social memory: E. Shils, *Tradition* (London, 1981); Z. Bauman, *Memories of Class: Pre-History and After Life of Class* (London, 1982); S. Nora, *Les lieux de la mémoire* (Paris, 1984); B. A. Smith, *Politics and Remembrance* (Princeton, 1985); P. Wright, *On Living in an Old Country* (London, 1985); F. Haug *Female Sexualization: a Collective Work of Memory* (tr. E. Carter, London, 1987).

30 On personal memory see R. Wollheim, *The Thread of Life* (Cambridge, 1984) and S. Shoemaker, 'Persons and Their Past', *American Philosophical Quarterly*, 7 (1970), 269–85.

31 See C. B. Martin and M. Deutscher, 'Remembering', *The Philosophical Review*, 75 (1966), pp. 161–96 and D. Wiggins, *Identity and Spatio-Temporal Continuity* (Oxford, 1967), esp. pp. 50 ff.

32 See H. Bergson, *Matter and Memory* (tr. N. M. Paul and W. S. Palmer, London, 1962).

33 B. Russell, *The Analysis of Mind* (London, 1921), pp. 166 ff.

34 A. R. Luria, *The Man with a Shattered World* (tr. L. Solotaroff, London, 1973).

35 See J. Laplanche and J. B. Pontalis, *The Language of Psychoanalysis* (tr. D. Nicholson-Smith, London, 1973).

36 S. Freud, 'Remembering, Repeating and Working Through' (1914), *Standard Edition*, XII, pp. 147–56.

37 On the role of narrative in psychoanalysis see M. Sherwood, *The Logic of Explanation in Psychoanalysis* (New York, 1969) and D. P. Spence, *Historical Truth and Narrative Truth: Meaning and Interpretation in Psychoanalysis* (New York, 1982).

38 See especially F. C. Bartlett, *Remembering* (Cambridge, 1932); J. Piaget and B. Inhelder, *Memory and Intelligence* (tr. A. J. Pomerans, London, 1973); A. Lieury, *La mémoire, résultats et théories* (Bruxelles, 1975).

39 On colour amnesia see M. Merleau-Ponty, *Phenomenology of Perception* (tr. C. Smith, London, 1962).

40 P. Winch, *The Idea of a Social Science* (London, 1958).

41 Ibid., pp. 57 ff.

42 See M. Oakeshott, *Rationalism in Politics* (London, 1962), especially pp. 61–9 and 119–29.

43 P. Winch, *Idea of a Social Science*, p. 58.

44 Ibid., pp. 59–60.

45 This example is discussed by C. Taylor, 'Interpretation and the Sciences of Man', in *Philosophy and the Human Sciences*, volume II (Cambridge, 1985), pp. 23 ff.

46 See M. Sahlins, 'La Pensée Bourgeoise: Western Society as Culture', in *Culture and Practical Reason* (Chicago, 1976), pp. 166–204.

47 See A. Martinet, *Eléments de linguistique générale* (Paris, 1960).

48 See H. E. Roberts, 'The Exquisite Slave: the Role of Clothes in the Making of the Victorian Woman', *Signs*, 2 (1977), pp. 554–69.

49 See M. Halbwachs, *Les cadres sociaux de la mémoire* (Paris, 1925); Halbwachs, *La mémoire collective* (Paris, 1950); see also by the same author, *La topographie légendaire des évangiles en terre sainte: Etude de mémoire collective* (Paris, 1941); 'La mémoire collective chez les musiciens', *Revue Philosophique*, 127 (1939), pp. 136–65.

50 M. Halbwachs, *Les cadres sociaux de la mémoire* (Paris, 1925), p. 392.

51 Ibid., p. 358.

52 Ibid., pp. 233–4.

53 See M. Bloch, *The Historian's Craft* (tr. R. Putnam, Manchester, 1954), pp. 40–1; for a review of Halbwachs (1925) see M. Bloch, 'Mémoire collective, tradition et coutume', *Revue de Synthèse Historique*, 40 (1925), pp. 73–83.

54 For corroborative remarks on this suggestion, with particular reference to the role of grandmothers in traditional societies, see D. Fabre and J. Lacroix, *La Tradition orale du conte occitan* (Paris, 1974), volume I, esp. pp. 111–15.

2 Commemorative ceremonies

1 On National Socialist rituals see H. T. Barden, *The Nuremberg Party Rallies, 1929–39* (London, 1967); J. P. Stern, *Hitler: The Führer and the People* (London, 1975); K. Vondung, *Magie und Manipulation, Ideologischer Kult und politische Religion des Nationalsozialismus* (Göttingen, 1971).

2 S. Lukes, 'Political Ritual and Social Integration', *Sociology*, 9 (1975), pp. 289–308, esp. p. 291.

3 On rites as having significance beyond the actual occasion see C. Geertz, 'Religion as a Cultural System', in D. Cutler (ed.), *The Religious Situation* (New York, 1968), pp. 639–87.

4 On Jewish liturgy see B. S. Childs, *Memory and Tradition in Israel* (London, 1962); I. Elbogen, *Der jüdische Gottesdienst in seiner geschichtlichen Entwicklung* (Hildesheim, 1962); N. N. Glatzer (ed.), *The Passover Haggadah* (New York, 1969); A. Z. Idelson, *Jewish Liturgy and its Development* (New York, 1967); B. Lewis, *History: Remembered, Recorded, Invented* (Princeton, 1975), pp. 47–8; S. Mowinckel, *Religion und Kultus* (Göttingen, 1953); J. Pederson, *Israel, its Life and Culture* (Oxford, 1940); J. Petuchowski, *Contributions to the Scientific Study of the Jewish Liturgy* (New York, 1970).

5 On Christian liturgy see O. Casel, *The Mystery of Christian Worship* (ed. B. Neunheuser, London, 1962); F. Clark, *Eucharistic Sacrifice and the Reformation* (Oxford, 1967); Y. M.-J. Congar, *Tradition and Traditions* (tr. M. Naseby and T. Rainborough, London, 1966); R. Guardini, *The Church and the Catholic, and the Spirit of the Liturgy* (tr. A. Lane, London, 1935); J. A. Jungmann, *Liturgische Erneuerung – Rückblick und Ausblick* (Kevalaer, 1962); Jungmann, *The Liturgy of the Word* (tr. H. E. Winstone, London, 1966).

6 On Muslim festivals see G. E. von Grunebaum, *Muhammadan Festivals* (New York, 1951) and B. Lewis, *History: Remembered, Recorded, Invented* (Princeton, 1975), p. 49.

7 See S. Freud, *Totem and Taboo*, in *Standard Edition*, vol. XII (tr. J. Strachey, with A. Freud, assisted by A. Strachey and A. Tyson, London 1953–66). On the Freudian interpretation of ritual see P. Ricoeur, 'Psychoanalysis and the Movement of Contemporary Culture', in P. Rabinow and W. M. Sullivan (eds.), *Interpretive Social Science* (Berkeley, 1979), pp. 301–9.

8 R. Wollheim, *The Sheep and the Ceremony* (Cambridge, 1979).

9 E. Durkheim, *The Elementary Forms of Religious Life* (tr. J. W. Swain, London, 1915), p. 225.

10 For the extension of the study of symbolism to political rituals see E. Shils and M. Young, 'The Meaning of the Coronation', *Sociological Review*, n.s. 1 (1953), pp. 63–81; L. Warner, *The Living and the Dead: A Study of the Symbolic Life of Americans* (New Haven, 1959).

11 For the use of political ritual as cognitive control see N. Birnbaum, 'Monarchies and Sociologists: a Reply to Professor Shils and Mr. Young', *Sociological Review*, n.s. 3 (1955), pp. 5–23; C. Geertz, 'Centers, Kings, and Charisma: Reflections on the Symbolism of Power', in J. Ben-David and T. N. Clark (eds.), *Culture and its Creators, Essays in Honor of Edward Shils*

(Chicago, 1977), pp. 150–71; S. Lukes, 'Political Ritual and Social Integration', *Sociology*, 9 (1975), pp. 289–308.

12 M. Bakhtin, *Rabelais and his World* (tr. H. Iswolsky, Cambridge, Mass., 1968), pp. 196–277.

13 For an elaboration of this position see D. Cannadine, 'The Context, Performance and Meaning of Ritual: the British Monarchy and the "Invention of Tradition", c. 1820–1977', in E. Hobsbawm and T. Ranger (eds.), *The Invention of Tradition* (Cambridge, 1983), pp. 101–64, especially 104–8.

14 For studies of political ritual in the early modern period see among others S. Anglo, *Spectacle, Pageantry and Early Tudor Policy* (Oxford, 1969); D. M. Bergeron, *English Civic Pageantry, 1558–1642* (London, 1971); P. Burke, *Popular Culture in Early Modern Europe* (London, 1978); R. E. Giesey, *The Royal Funeral Ceremony in Renaissance France* (Geneva, 1960); E. Muir, *Civic Ritual in Renaissance Venice* (Princeton, 1981); S. Orgel, *The Illusion of Power: Political Theater in the English Renaissance* (Berkeley, 1975); R. Strong, *Splendour at Court: Renaissance Spectacle and Illusion* (London, 1973); F. A. Yates, *The Valois Tapestries* (London, 1959).

15 For studies of political ritual in the modern period see especially E. Hobsbawm and T. Ranger (eds.), *The Invention of Tradition* (Cambridge, 1983); see also M. Agulhon, 'Esquisse pour une archéologie de la république: l'allégorie civique féminine', *Annales*, 28 (1973), pp. 5–34; Agulhon, *Marianne into Battle: Republican Imagery and Symbolism in France, 1789–1880* (tr. J. Lloyd, Cambridge, 1981); R. Bocock, *Ritual in Industrial Society* (London, 1974); G. Kernodle, *From Art to Theater* (Chicago, 1944); C. Lane, *The Rites of Rulers: Ritual in Industrial Society – the Soviet Case* (Cambridge, 1981); G. L. Mosse, 'Caesarism, Circuses and Monuments', *Journal of Contemporary History*, 6 (1971), pp. 167–82; G. L. Mosse, 'Mass Politics and the Political Liturgy of Nationalism', in E. Kamenka (ed.), *Nationalism: the Nature and Evolution of an Ideal* (London, 1976), pp. 39–54; M. Novak, *Choosing our King* (New York, 1974); C. Rearick, 'Festivals and Politics: The Michelet Centennial of 1898', in W. Laqueur and G. L. Mosse (eds.), *Historians in Politics* (London, 1974), pp. 59–78; C. Rearick, 'Festivals in Modern France: the Experience of the Third Republic', *Journal of Contemporary History*, 12 (1977), pp. 435–60; R. Samson, 'La fête de Jeanne d'Arc en 1894: controverse et célébration', *Revue d'Histoire Moderne et Contemporaine*, 20 (1973), pp. 444–63; L. Warner, *The Living and the Dead: a Study of the Symbolic Life of Americans* (New Haven, 1959).

16 On invented tradition in the Third Republic and Wilhelmine Germany see E. Hobsbawm, 'Mass-Producing Traditions: Europe, 1870-1914', in E. Hobsbawm and T. Ranger (eds), *The Invention of Tradition* (Cambridge, 1983), pp. 263–307, especially 269 ff. and 273 ff. and T. Nipperdey, 'Nationalidee und Nationaldenkmal in Deutschland im 19. Jahrhundert', *Historische Zeitschrift*, 208 (1968), 529–85.

17 See B. Lewis, *History: Remembered, Recorded, Invented* (Princeton, 1975), pp. 3–41.

18 E. Leach, 'Ritualisation in Man in Relation to Conceptual and Social Development', in J. Huxley (ed.), *Philosophical Transactions of the Royal Society of London*, Series B, vol. 251 (1966), especially pp. 405–6.

19 See R. A. Rappaport, 'The Obvious Aspects of Ritual', *Cambridge Anthropology*, 2 (1974), p. 32.

20 On the theme of surplus meaning see P. Ricoeur, *Interpretation Theory: Discourse and the Surplus of Meaning* (Fort Worth, 1976). For a consideration of the dramatic changes in the treatment of the Orestes myth, see K. von Fritz, *Antike und moderne Tragödie* (Berlin, 1962), pp. 113 ff; for the Antigone myth see G. Steiner, *Antigones* (Oxford, 1984); for a detailed general treatment of the way in which Western culture has transformed its myths, with particular references to the Prometheus myth, see H. Blumenberg, *Work on Myth* (tr. R. M. Wallace, Cambridge, Mass., 1985).

21 See A. Baumstark, 'Das Gesetz der Erhaltung des Alten in liturgisch hochwertiger Zeit', *Jahrbuch für Liturgiewissenschaft*, 7 (1927), pp. 1–23.

22 See A. Z. Idelson, *Jewish Liturgy and its Development* (New York, 1932), p. 310; W. Leslav, *Falasha Anthology. The Black Jews of Ethiopia* (New York, 1951), p. 124; S. Strizower, *The Children of Israel. The Beni Israel of Bombay* (Oxford, 1971), p. 14.

23 My account of the formal features of ritual action is much indebted to two classic papers: M. Bloch, 'Symbols, Song, Dance and Features of Articulation', *Archives Européennes de Sociologie*, 15 (1974), pp. 55–81; and R. A. Rappaport, 'The Obvious Aspects of Ritual', *Cambridge Anthropology*, 2 (1974), pp. 3–68. Rappaport has developed his views on this subject in a series of articles: 'Ritual, Sanctity and Cybernetics', *American Anthropologist*, 73 (1971), pp. 59–76; 'The Sacred in Human Evolution', *Annual Review of Ecology and Systematics*, 2 (1971), pp. 23–44; 'Liturgy and Lies', *International Yearbook for Sociology of Knowledge and Religion*, 10 (1976), pp. 75–104; 'Concluding Comments on Ritual and Reflexivity', *Semiotica*, 30 (1980), pp. 181–93. For comment on the formal features of ritual see also A. F. C. Wallace, *Religion: an Anthropological View* (New York, 1966); V. Turner, *The Forest of Symbols* (Ithaca, 1967); Turner, *The Ritual Process* (Chicago, 1969); Turner, *Dramas, Fields and Metaphors* (Ithaca, 1974); J. Skorupski, *Symbol and Theory: a Philosophical Study of Theories of Religion in Social Anthropology* (Cambridge, 1976); S. J. Tambiah, 'A Performative Approach to Ritual', *Proceedings of the British Academy*, 65 (1979), pp. 113–69.

24 For a discussion of performatives see J. L. Austin, *How to do Things with Words* (Oxford, 1962); Austin, 'Performative Utterances', in *Philosophical Papers*, 2nd ed., J. O. Urmson and G. T. Warnock (eds.) (Oxford, 1970); J. R. Searle, *Speech Acts* (Cambridge, 1969). For a discussion of performatives in ritual see R. Finnegan, 'How to do Things with Words: Performative Utterances among the Limba of Sierra Leone', *Man*, 4 (1969), pp. 537–51; J. Ladrière, 'The Performativity of Liturgical Language', *Concilium*, 2 (1973), pp. 50–62; H. Lavondes, 'Magie et langage', *L'Homme*, 3 (1963), pp. 109–17;

S. J. Tambiah, 'A Performative Approach to Ritual', *Proceedings of the British Academy*, 65 (1979), pp. 113–69.

25 See G. van der Leeuw, *Religion in Essence and Manifestation* (tr. J. E. Turner, Gloucester, Mass., 1967), especially pp. 405–11.

26 Some comments on bodily performatives are made by M. Bloch and R. A. Rappaport.

27 R. Jakobson, 'Grammatical Parallelism and its Russian Facet', *Language*, 42 (1966), p. 399.

28 On canonical parallelism see particularly J. J. Fox, 'On Binary Categories and Primary Symbols', in R. Willis (ed.), *The Interpretation of Symbolism* (London, 1975), pp. 99–132; Fox, 'Roman Jakobson and the Comparative Study of Parallelism', in D. Armstrong and C. H. van Schooneveld (eds.), *Roman Jakobson. Echoes of his Scholarship* (Lisse, 1977), pp. 59–90; see also L. I. Newman and W. Popper, *Studies in Biblical Parallelism* (California, 1918–23); S. Gevirtz, *Patterns in the Early Poetry of Israel* (Chicago, 1963); G. A. Reichard, *Prayer: The Compulsive Word* (Seattle, 1944); W. Steinitz, *Der Parallelismus in der finnisch=karelischen Volksdichtung* (Helsinki, 1934).

29 M. Bloomfield, *Rig-Veda Repetitions* (Cambridge, Mass., 1916), p. 5.

30 For a discussion of this aspect of ritual see especially M. Bloch, 'Symbols, Song, Dance and Features of Articulation', *Archives Européennes de Sociologie*, 15 (1974), pp. 55–81.

31 P. de Man, 'Literary History and Literary Modernity', *Daedalus*, 99 (1970), pp. 384–404.

32 Ibid., pp. 388–9.

33 See H. Lefebvre, *Everyday Life in the Modern World* (tr. S. Rabinovitch, London, 1971). For a discussion of postmodernism and attitudes to history see F. Jameson, 'The Cultural Logic of Capital', *New Left Review*, 146 (1984), pp. 53–93.

34 T. Mann, 'Freud and the Future', tr. H. T. Lowe-Porter, in P. Meisel (ed.), *Freud* (Englewood Cliffs, N. J., 1981), pp. 45–60.

35 See S. Zukin, 'Ten Years of the New Urban Sociology', *Theory and Society*, 9 (1980), pp. 575–601.

36 For an investigation of the experience of modernity which brings out these features see M. Berman, *All that is Solid Melts into Air* (New York, 1982), and the discussion of this book in P. Anderson, 'Modernity and Revolution', *New Left Review*, 144 (1984), pp. 96–113.

37 On calendrical repetition see H. Hubert and M. Mauss, 'La représentation du temps dans la religion et la magie', *Mélanges d'Histoire des Religions* (Paris, 1909), pp. 189–229; M. Eliade, *The Myth of Eternal Return* (New York, 1954); Eliade, *The Sacred and the Profane* (New York, 1959); Eliade, *Myth and Reality* (New York, 1963); R. Caillois, *L'Homme et le sacré* (Paris, 1950); G. Dumézil, 'Temps et mythes', *Recherches Philosophiques*, 5 (1935–6), pp. 235–51; R. Marchal, 'Le retour éternal', *Archives Philosophiques*, 3 (1925), pp. 55–91.

38 A. J. Wensinck, 'The Semitic New Year and the Origin of Eschatology', *Acta Orientalia*, I (Lund, 1923), pp. 158–99.

39 H. Hubert and M. Mauss, 'La représentation du temps dans la religion et la magie', *Mélanges d'Histoire des Religions* (Paris, 1909), p. 206.

40 See S. J. Tambiah, 'The Magical Power of Words', *Man*, 3 (1968), pp. 175–208.

41 M. Bloch, 'Symbols, Song, Dance and Features of Articulation', *Archives Européennes de Sociologie*, 15 (1974), pp. 77–8.

42 R. Caillois, *Man, Play, and Games* (tr. M. Barash, London, 1962), pp. 108–9.

43 D. Forde, *The Ethnography of the Yuma Indians* (Berkeley, 1931).

44 See E. Canetti, *Crowds and Power* (tr. C. Stewart, London, 1962), pp. 313–14.

45 L. Lévy-Bruhl, *Primitives and the Supernatural* (tr. L. A. Clare, New York, 1973), pp. 123–4.

46 On Shiite festivals see E. Canetti, *Crowds and Power*, pp. 171–81.

47 On liturgical gesture and biblical reference see J. Daniélou, *The Bible and the Liturgy* (London, 1956).

3   Bodily practices

1 See M. Mead, *Continuities in Cultural Evolution* (New Haven, 1964), esp. pp. 45–6.

2 On the upright posture see E. Straus, *Essays in Phenomenological Psychology* (London, 1966), pp. 137–65.

3 See G. Lakoff and M. Johnson, *Metaphors We Live By* (New York, 1980), esp. pp. 15–20 and 56–7.

4 See P. Ricoeur, *Interpretation Theory: Discourse and the Surplus of Meaning* (Fort Worth, 1976), pp. 42 ff.

5 For the impact of writing on social memory see especially J. Goody, *The Domestication of the Savage Mind* (Cambridge, 1977); J. Goody and I. P. Watt, 'The Consequences of Literacy', *Comparative Studies in History and Society*, 5 (1963), pp. 304–45; J. Goody, 'Literacy and the Non-Literate', in R. Disch (ed.), *The Future of Literacy* (Englewood Cliffs, 1973); J. Goody, 'Mémoire et apprentissage dans les sociétés avec et sans écriture: la transmission du Bagre', *L'Homme*, 17 (1977), pp. 29–52; but see also E. L. Eisenstein, 'Some Conjectures about the Impact of Printing on Western Society and Thought', *Journal of Modern History*, 40 (1968), pp. 1–56; I. J. Gelb, *A Study of Writing* (Chicago, 1952); E. A. Havelock, *Origins of Western Literacy* (Toronto, 1976); Havelock, 'The Preliteracy of the Greeks', *New Literary History*, 8 (1977), pp. 369–92; Havelock, *The Literate Revolution in Greece and its Cultural Consequences* (Princeton, 1982).

6 For the effect of rhythm on memory see especially M. Jousse, 'Études de psychologie linguistique. Le style oral rhythmique et mnémotechnique chez les verbo-moteurs', *Archives de Philosophie*, vol. II, 4 (1924), pp. 1–240; but see also E. A. Havelock, *Preface to Plato* (Cambridge, Mass., 1963).

7 On literary and cultural scepticism see J. Goody and I. P. Watt, 'The

Consequences of Literacy', *Comparative Studies in History and Society*, 5 (1963), pp. 304–45.

8 On writing and habit memory see S. Butler, *Life and Habit* (London, 1878), pp. 6–7.

9 M. Foucault, *Discipline and Punish. The Birth of the Prison* (tr. A. Sheridan, London, 1977), p. 152.

10 On the cinematic institution see particularly C. Metz, *Le Signifiant imaginaire* (Paris, 1977).

11 D. Efron, *Gesture and Environment* (New York, 1941).

12 A. di Jorio, *Mimica degli Antichi Investigata nel Gestire Napoletano* (Napoli, 1832).

13 K. Sittl, *Die Gebärden der Griechen und Römer* (Leipzig, 1890).

14 D. Erasmus, *De civilitate morum puerilium* (Basel, 1530).

15 N. Elias, *The Civilizing Process* (tr. E. Jephcott, London, 1978).

16 On stylised consumption see P. Bourdieu, *Distinction* (tr. R. Nice, London, 1984).

17 Comte de Saint-Simon, *Projets de Gouvernement du Duc de Bourgogne* (1714–15), ed. P. Mesnard (Paris, 1860) and *Mémoires* (London, 1788).

18 See R. Mousnier, *Social Hierarchies: 1450 to the Present* (tr. P. Evans, London, 1973); and R. Mousnier, *Les Institutions de la France sous la monarchie absolue, 1598–1789* (Paris, 1974).

19 M. Proust, *Remembrance of Things Past* (tr. C. K. Scott Moncrieff and T. Kilmartin, London, 1981), vol. III, p. 1006.

20 La Roque, *Traité de la Noblesse* (Paris, 1735), Préface, quoted in Mousnier (1974), p. 101.

21 La Bruyère, *Characters* (tr. J. Stewart, Harmondsworth, 1970), p. 133.

22 M. Foucault, *Power/Knowledge* (selected interviews and other writings, ed. and tr. C. Gordon, Brighton, 1980), p. 147.

23 See R. Hatton, 'Louis XIV. At the Court of the Sun King', in A. G. Dickens (ed.), *The Courts of Europe: Politics, Patronage and Royalty, 1400–1800* (London, 1977), pp. 233–62.

24 On the concept of symbolic capital see P. Bourdieu, *Distinction: A Social Critique of the Judgement of Taste* (tr. R. Nice, London, 1984).

25 M. Proust, *Remembrance of Things Past* (tr. C. K. Scott Moncrieff and T. Kilmartin, London, 1981), vol. I, pp. 791–2.

26 On the distinction between 'knowing' and 'recognizing' see further P. Bourdieu, 'Remarques provisoires sur la perception du corps', *Actes de la Recherche en Sciences Sociales*, 14 (1977), pp. 51–4; Bourdieu, 'La production de la croyance: contribution à une économie des biens symboliques', *Actes de la Recherche en Sciences Sociales*, 13 (1977), pp. 3–44; P. Bourdieu and J. C. Passeron, *Reproduction in Education, Society and Culture* (tr. R. Nice, London, 1977); Bourdieu, *Outline of a Theory of Practice* (tr. R. Nice, London, 1977); Bourdieu, *Distinction* (tr. R. Nice, London, 1984).

27 D. Sudnow, *Ways of the Hand: the Organization of Improvised Conduct* (London, 1978), pp. 30–3.

28 Ibid., pp. 12–13.
29 W. Dewey, *Human Nature and Conduct: an Introduction to Social Psychology* (London, 1922), pp. 24–5.
30 M. Merleau-Ponty, *Phenomenology of Perception* (tr. C. Smith, London, 1962), p. 144.
31 The classic accounts of this turning-point in the history of hermeneutics are to be found in H.-G. Gadamer, *Truth and Method* (London, 1975); E. Betti, 'Zur Grundlegung einer allgemeinen Auslegungslehre', in *Festschrift für Ernst Rabel* (Tübingen, 1954), vol. II, pp. 79–168; E. Betti, *Allgemeine Auslegungslehre als Methodik der Geisteswissenschaften* (Tübingen, 1967).
32 See P. Ricoeur, *Hermeneutics and the Human Sciences* (tr. J. B. Thompson, Cambridge, 1981), p. 91.
33 On the analogy between legal and theological hermeneutics see E. Betti, 'Zur Grundlegung einer allgemeinen Auslegungslehre', in *Festschrift für Ernst Rabel* (Tübingen, 1954), vol. II, p. 145; J. Wach, *Das Verstehen* (Hildesheim, 1966), vol. II, pp. 60–1, 183 ff.
34 On medieval interpretations of Roman Law see P. Koschaker, *Europa und das Römische Recht* (München, 1966); Q. Skinner, *The Foundations of Modern Political Thought* (Cambridge, 1978), vol. I, pp. 9–12.
35 On legal humanists and the study of Roman Law see D. R. Kelley, 'Legal Humanism and the Sense of History', *Studies in the Renaissance*, 13 (1966), pp. 184–99; Kelley, *Foundations of Modern Historical Scholarship: Language, Law and History in the French Renaissance* (New York, 1970); Kelley, 'Vera Philosophia: the Philosophical Significance of Renaissance Jurisprudence', *The Journal of the History of Philosophy*, 14 (1976), pp. 267–79; Q. Skinner, I, pp. 105–6, II, 269–72, 290–3.
36 On medieval interpretation of the Bible see W. Schwarz, *Principles and Problems of Biblical Translation* (Cambridge, 1955); Q. Skinner, *The Foundations of Modern Political Thought* (Cambridge, 1978), I, pp. 208–9.
37 On the humanist interpretation of the Bible see W. Schwarz, *Principles and Problems of Biblical Translation* (Cambridge, 1955); Q. Skinner, *The Foundations of Modern Political Thought* (Cambridge, 1978), I, pp. 209–12.
38 E. Panofsky, *Renaissance and Renascences in Western Art* (Stockholm, 1960), pp. 110–11.
39 On the development of critical reading see especially J. H. Franklin, *Jean Bodin and the Sixteenth-Century Revolution in the Methodology of Law and History* (New York, 1963), and J. G. A. Pocock, 'The Origins of Study of the Past', *Comparative Studies in History and Society*, 4 (1962), pp. 209–46.
40 On the double strategy of etherealisation and materialisation see R. Keat, 'The Human Body in Social Theory: Reich, Foucault and the Repressive Hypothesis', *Radical Philosophy*, 42 (1986), pp. 24–32.

Subject index

acting out, 25–6
amnesia, 27

bodily practices, 10–13, 72–104
  and ceremonies of the body, 84–7
  and cinema, 78
  and court etiquette, 84–8
  and East European Jewish gestures,
    79–82
  and gestures, 79–82
  as mnemonics, 102
  and performativeness, 59
  and proprieties of the body, 82–4
  and Southern Italian gestures, 79–82
  and table manners, 82–4
  and techniques of the body, 79–82
  and writing, 76–8

calendrical rites, 65–6
ceremonial privileges, 86–7
clothing conventions, 32–4
cognitive memory, 22, 27–8, 35, 87–8
  and encoding, 27–8
  and semantic coding, 27
  and verbal coding, 27
  and visual coding, 27
commemorative ceremonies, 7–10, 41–71
  and biblical quotation, 70
  and Cyrus, 52
  and calendrical ceremonies, 45
  and capitalism, 63–5
  and Christian festivals, 46–7
  and the crucifixion, 46–7
  and Deuteronomy, 46
  and Easter, 66
  and Exodus, 46
  and Hanukka, 46
  and Husain, 69, 70
  and Islamic festivals, 47–8
  and Jewish festivals, 45–6

  and Kachin, 67
  and the Koran, 66
  and the Last Supper, 47, 48
  and Luapala, 68
  and Masada, 52
  and Purim, 46
  and Ramadan, 47, 48
  and Sabbath, 46
  and Seder, 46
  and Shevouth, 46
  and Shiite festivals, 69–70
  and Sukkoth, 46
  and the Third Reich, 41–3
  and the Third Republic, 51
  and Trobrianders, 67
  and Wilhelmine Germany, 52
  and Yuma Indians, 68

forgetting, 14–15, 61–2
French Revolution, 4, 6–13
Futurism, 62

habit, 5, 29–31, 34, 83, 93–5
  and habit-memory, 22–5, 28–9, 36, 84,
    88
  and individual habits, 34–5
  and social habits, 34–6
handwriting, 76–8
hereditary transmission, 87
hermeneutics, 4, 95–7
  and biblical interpretation, 98–9
  and *Geisteswissenschaften*, 101
  and humanism, 98–100
  and legal interpretation, 96–8
  and the linguistic turn, 101
  and Roman law, 97–8
  and theological interpretation, 96–8
  historical reconstruction, 13–14
historiography, 13–16
  and the Crusades, 15–16

and nationalism, 16
  and totalitarianism, 14–15
horizon of expectations, 2–3, 6, 11–12

incorporating practices, 72–3, 77, 101–2
informal narratives, 17–21, 26
inscribing practices, 73, 78, 101–2
invention of tradition, 51–2, 103

jazz, 91–3

modernity, 61–2
myth, 53–7
  and the Don Juan myth, 54–5
  and the Faust myth, 54–5
  and mythic identification, 63
  and the Orestes–Electra myth, 55–6

performativeness, 4, 58–9
personal memory, 22, 25–6, 35
postures, 73
psychoanalysis, 27–8, 35
psychology, 27–8, 35

repetition compulsion, 25–6
ritual, 44–5
  and canonical parallelism, 60
  and carnivals, 50
  and gestural repetition, 68–71
  and the invention of ritual, 51–2, 63
  and oedipal conflict, 49
  and the pathology of ritual, 49
  and the psychoanalytic interpretation
    of ritual, 48–9
  and ritual blessings, 58
  and ritual curses, 58
  and ritual formalism, 59–61
  and ritual invariance, 57
  and ritual oaths, 58
  and ritual pronouns, 58–9
  and ritual recitation, 66–8
  and ritual re-enactment, 53, 61, 65, 72
  and the sociological interpretation of
    ritual, 49–50
  and symbolic representation, 53
  and verbal re-enactment, 66–8

social codes, 32–6, 90
social memory, 1, 3, 36–8, *passim*
  and the alphabet, 74–5
  and the assumptions of 1914, 18
  and autobiography, 18–20
  and bodily practices, 10–13, 72–104
  and brigandage, 20–1
  and capitalism, 63–5
  and Christian festivals, 46–7

and clothing conventions, 10–12, 32–4
and commemorative ceremonies, 7–10,
  41–71
and coronations, 8–9
and dynastic succession, 7–9
and etiquette at court, 84–8
and the French Revolution, 4, 6–13
and genealogies, 85–6
and generational continuity, 3, 38–9
and generic expectations, 11–12
and gestures, 79–82
and grandparents, 38–9
and the Great War, 20–1
and habit, 5, 29–31, 34, 83, 93–5
and handwriting, 76–8
and hereditary transmission, 85–6
and hermeneutics, 96–101
and historical reconstruction, 13–14
and the history of the Crusades, 15–16
and the horizon of expectations, 2–3,
  6, 11–12
and incorporation, 72–3, 77, 101–2
and informal histories, 17–21
and inscription, 73, 78, 101–2
and the invention of tradition, 51–2,
  103
and Islamic festivals, 47–8
and Jewish festivals, 45–6
and legitimation, 1, 3, 7, 90–1
and memoirs, 18–20
and metaphors, 74
and modernity, 61–2
and myth, 53–7
and national identity, 16
and the Nuremberg Trials, 7
and oral history, 17–19
and the oral history of dominant
  groups, 19
and the oral history of subordinate
  groups, 19–20
and the political education of ruling
  group, 17–18
and the political memory of ruling
  groups, 18
and political records, 17–18
and postures, 73–4
and regicide, 7–9
and rhythm, 76
and scepticism, 76
and symbolic capital, 87
and table manners, 82–4
and totalitarian regimes, 14–15
and tradition, 4, 95–101
and the transmission of property, 9–10
and the trial by fiat of successor
  regimes, 7–9

social memory *cont.*
    and the trial of Louis XVI, 7–8
    and the unconscious, 1
    and villages, 17

    and the Wars of Religion, 18
    and writing, 75–6
social rules, 29–31, 34–6

Name index

Aeschylus, 55, 56
Agulhon, 110
Alexander, 62
Anderson, 112
Anglo, 110
Aristotle, 55
Austin, 111

Bakhtin, 50, 106, 110
Barden, 109
Bartlett, 108
Bauman, 105, 107
Baumstark, 111
Bell, 107
Berger, 107
Bergeron, 110
Bergson, 23, 108
Berlin, 106
Berman, 112
Betti, 115
Birnbaum, 109
Bloch, Marc, 39, 106, 108
Bloch, Maurice, 111, 112, 113
Bloomfield, 60, 112
Blumenberg, 111
Boissevain, 107
Bourdieu, 84, 114
Boyers, 105
Buck, 106
Burke, Edmund, 11
Burke, Peter, 110
Butler, 114
Butterfield, 107

Caesar, 62
Caillois, 68, 112, 113
Camus, 8, 106
Canetti, 113
Cannadine, 110
Casel, 109

Castiglione, 82
Chaplin, 92
Charles I, 9
Christ, 62, 66, 68
Chesneaux, 107
Childs, 109
Cicero, 39
Clark, 109
Clytemnestra, 56
Collingwood, 106
Comte, 37
Congar, 109

Daniélou, 113
De Man, 61, 62, 112
Della Casa, 82
Deutscher, 107
Dewey, 93, 115
Di Jorio, 80, 114
Dilthey, 96
Dumézil, 112
Durkheim, 38, 50, 103, 109

Efron, 79, 80, 81, 114
Eisenstein, 113
Elbogen, 109
Eliade, 112
Elias, 83, 84, 114
Ennew, 107
Erasmus, 82, 83, 99, 114
Euripides, 55

Fabre, 108
Finnegan, 111
Forde, 68, 113
Foucault, 77, 86, 114
Fox, 112
Franklin, J. H., 115
Franklin, S. H., 107
Freud, 26, 48, 49, 62, 108, 109

Friedl, 107
Fussell, 20, 107

Gabrieli, 106
Gadamer, 115
Geertz, 109
Gelb, 113
Gevirtz, 112
Giesey, 110
Glatzer, 109
Goldstein, 106
Goody, 113
Guardini, 109

Halbwachs, 36, 37, 38, 105, 108
Harrison, 107
Hatton, 114
Haug, 105, 107
Havelock, 113
Henri III, 8
Henri IV, 8, 85
Hitler, 41, 42
Hirsch, 106
Hobsbawn, 105, 110
Holt, 106
Hunt, 106
Hubert, 112, 113

Idelson, 109, 111
Inhelder, 108

Jakobson, 60, 112
Jameson, 105, 112
Jardine, 107
Johnson, 113
Joll, 107
Jousse, 113
Jungmann, 109

Kamenka, 110
Kant, 7, 106
Kantorowicz, 106
Keat, 115
Kelley, 115
Kern, 106
Kernodle, 110
Kirchheimer, 106
Kohli-Kunz, 106
Koschaker, 115
Koselleck, 105

Lacroix, 108
Ladrière, 111
Lakoff, 113
Lane, 110
Laplanche, 108

Laqueur, 110
Lavondes, 111
La Bruyère, 85, 114
La Roque, 85, 114
La Salle, 77
Leach, 53, 111
Lefebvre, 62, 112
Leslav, 111
Levi, 20, 107
Lévi-Strauss, 53, 103
Lévy-Bruhl, 69, 113
Lewis, 106, 109, 110
Lieury, 108
Louis XIV, 85
Louis XVI, 7, 8, 9
Lowenthal, 105
Lukes, 44, 109, 110
Luria, 24, 108

Macfarlane, 107
MacIntyre, 107
Malinowski, 103
Mann, 61, 62, 63, 112
Manning, Cardinal, 80
Marchal, 112
Martin, 107
Martinet, 108
Marx, 63
Mattelart, 105
Mauss, 112, 113
Mead, 113
Meinecke, 106
Merleau-Ponty, 95, 108, 115
Metz, 78, 114
Mill, 29
Miltiades, 62
Mosse, 110
Mousnier, 114
Mowinckel, 109
Muhammad, 47
Muir, 110

Newby, 107
Newman, 112
Nipperdey, 110
Nora, 105, 107
Novak, 110

Oakeshot, 11, 29, 30, 31, 34, 106, 108
Oliphant, Mrs, 33
Orgel, 110
Orwell, 115

Panofsky, 100, 115
Passeron, 114
Pederson, 109

Perrault, 39
Petuchowski, 109
Piaget, 108
Pindar, 55
Plato, 96
Pocock, 115
Pontalis, 108
Popper, 112
Proust, 2, 3, 17, 88, 89, 90, 93, 94, 105,
    107, 114

Quintilian, 80

Rabinow, 109
Ranger, 105, 110
Rappaport, 111
Rearick, 110
Reill, 106
Reuchlin, 99
Ricoeur, 96, 109, 111, 113, 115
Ritter, 106
Roberts, 108
Rossi, 107
Russell, 23, 108

Sahlins, 29, 32, 34, 35, 108
Saint-Simon, Comte de, 84, 85, 114
Samson, 110
Saussure, 32
Schieder, 105, 107
Schleiermacher, 95, 96
Schiller, 105
Schulte, 107
Schwarz, 115
Searle, 111
Sennett, 106, 107
Sherwood, 26, 108
Shils, 105, 107, 109
Shoemaker, 107
Simonides, 55
Sittl, 80, 114
Sivan, 106
Skinner, 115

Skorupski, 111
Smith, 105, 107
Solzhenitsyn, 15
Sophocles, 55, 56
Spence, 26, 108
Stallybrass, 106
Steiner, 105, 111
Steinitz, 112
Stern, 109
Stesichoros, 55
Straus, 113
Strizower, 111
Strong, 110
Sudnow, 91, 92, 93, 94, 114
Sullivan, 109

Tambiah, 111, 112, 113
Taylor, 108
Terkel, 20
Turner, 111

Valla, 99
Van der Leeuw, 112
Vondung, 109
Von Fritz, 111
Von Grunebaum, 109

Wach, 115
Walzer, 106
Wallace, 111
Warner, 109, 110
Watt, 113
Wensinck, 113
White, 106
Wiggins, 107
Winch, 29, 30, 31, 32, 34, 35, 108
Wollheim, 49, 107, 109
Wright, 105, 107

Yates, 110
Young, 109

Zukin, 112